OXFORD INDIA SHORT INTRODUCTIONS

MUGHAL PAINTING

The Oxford India Short Introductions are concise, stimulating, and accessible guides to different aspects of India. Combining authoritative analysis, new ideas, and diverse perspectives, they discuss subjects which are topical yet enduring, as also emerging areas of study and debate.

OXFORD
INDIA SHORT
INTRODUCTIONS

MUGHAL
PAINTING

SOM PRAKASH VERMA

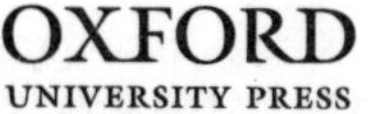

OXFORD
UNIVERSITY PRESS

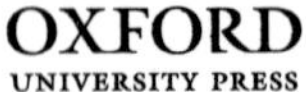

OXFORD
UNIVERSITY PRESS

Oxford University Press is a department of the University of Oxford.
It furthers the University's objective of excellence in research, scholarship,
and education by publishing worldwide. Oxford is a registered trademark of
Oxford University Press in the UK and in certain other countries

Published in India by
Oxford University Press
YMCA Library Building, 1 Jai Singh Road, New Delhi 110 001, India

© Oxford University Press 2014

The moral rights of the author have been asserted

First Edition published in 2014

ISBN-13: 978-0-19-945113-5
ISBN-10: 0-19-945113-3

Typeset in 11/15.6 Bembo Std
by Excellent Laser Typesetters, Pitampura, Delhi 110 034
Printed in India at G.H. Prints Pvt Ltd, New Delhi 110 020

To
Dr (Smt.) Kapila Vatsyayan

Contents

Figures

Note: Plates 1–9 and 11–14 are credited to the © Victoria and Albert Museum, London. Plate 10 is credited to the © Habibganj Collection, Aligarh Muslim University, Aligarh.

Preface

Mughal art reinterpreted both Islamic and Indian aesthetics, unlike the conventional art of India and Persia. The Mughal patrons and painters were aware of the various new art concepts in vogue in contemporary Europe and they skilfully adopted some of these concepts in their paintings. Their devoted endeavour and ability towards adoption and adaptation gave rise to the Mughal School of Art which subsequently also led to the modernization of Indian art. The Mughal Emperor Jahangir's (r. 1605–27) humanistic vision in art steered a final change in Mughal taste and aesthetics which brushed aside the past and present of Persian and Indian paintings.

A book on Mughal painting can never do complete justice to the wide thematic range of Mughal school of painting that offers the richest details on artists, their patrons, and work. This important school of Indian art brought together diverse cultures and created a strong sense of pride in Indian heritage among the Indians.

Acknowledgements

I thank the following institutions for permitting me to reproduce the miniatures from their collections: Khuda Bakhsh Oriental Public Library, Patna; Rampur Raza Library, Rampur; and Habibganj Collection, Maulana Azad Library, Aligarh Muslim University, Aligarh.

I express my special gratitude to Professor Emeritus Irfan Habib to whom I have always turned for inspiration and information. I am grateful to Professors Pushpa Prasad and Shireen Moosvi and Drs Syed Ali Nadeem Rezavi and Ishrat Alam, amongst others. Special thanks are due to Ghulam Mujtaba, a veteran photographer who prepared the excellent digital images, and to Syed Nadeem Husain, who helped me to prepare the word files with competence.

I record my sincere gratitude to my family and to Dr Smriti Prasad, and her daughters, Astha and Ami.

Finally, I am thankful to Oxford University Press, New Delhi, for making this work accessible to a wider readership.

Som Prakash Verma

Abbreviations

A'in	*A'in-i Akbari*
BAAC	Birla Academy of Art & Culture, Kolkata (formerly Calcutta)
BKB	Bharat Kala Bhavan, Banaras Hindu University, Varanasi
BLO	Bodleian Library, Oxford
BM	British Museum and Library, London
BMB	Brooklyn Museum, Brooklyn, New York
CACA	A.C. Ardeshir Collection, Mumbai
CAG	Ajit Ghosh Collection, Kolkata
CAM	Cincinnati Art Museum, Ohio
CBL	Chester Beatty Library, Dublin
CBQ	Collection of Bernard Quaritch, Paris

CK	Keir Collection, Pontresina
CMA	Cleveland Museum of Art, Cleveland
CSM	Chhatrapati Shivaji Maharaj Vastu Sangrahalaya, Mumbai
CW	Wantage Collection, Victoria and Albert Museum, London
FAM	Fogg Art Museum/Harvard Art Museum, Cambridge, Massachusetts
FGA	Freer Gallery of Art, Washington, D.C.
HC	Habibganj Collection, Maulana Azad Library, Aligarh Muslim University
IL	Imperial Library, Gulistan Palace Library, Tehran
IM	Indian Museum, Kolkata
IOL	Indian Office Library, The British Library, London
LACM	Los Angeles County Museum of Art, Los Angeles
MduL	Muséee du Louvre, Paris
MG	Muséee Guimet, Paris
MMA	The Metropolitan Museum of Art, New York
NM	National Museum, New Delhi

OPL	Khuda Bakhsh Oriental Public Library (formerly Khuda Bakhsh Library, Bankipore), Patna
RAS	Royal Asiatic Society, London
RRL	Rampur Raza Library, Rampur
RLWC	Royal Library, Windsor Castle, London
SMOA	State Museum of Oriental Art, Moscow
SMPG	The Baroda Museum and Picture Gallery, Baroda
SMS	Maharaja Sawai Man Singh II Museum, Jaipur
SOAS	School of Oriental and African Studies, London
VA	Victoria and Albert Museum, London
VM	Victoria Memorial Hall, Kolkata
VMB	Volkerkunde Museum, Berlin
WAM	Walters Art Museum, Baltimore

Introduction

Painting, Patrons, and Painters

Mughal painting originated from the book-painting tradition practised at the courts of Muslim rulers in India since the fifteenth century. Deeply influenced by a diverse mixture of cultural, regional, and artistic traditions, Mughal painting developed into one of the richest and most productive schools in the history of Indian and Islamic painting. The Mughal school reveals an assimilation of traits of the various art schools that flourished in India, Persia, Central Asia, and Europe. However, the eclectic Mughal style that developed during the sixteenth and seventeenth centuries was completely different from the contemporary or near contemporary schools of art. Thus, the nomenclature

'Indo-Persian' given to this particular style is misleading. Similarly, the impression that the products of this school are 'court-paintings' is also incorrect. The Mughal paintings encompass an immense wealth of information on contemporary day-to-day life and portray the common people in their environment and surroundings. It is an art of a very high order. These paintings even depict non-Islamic mythological and religious themes and undoubtedly constitute the most extensive source of visual reconstruction of the life, work, and manners of contemporary society. The Mughal painters' interest extended to the environment, and plants and animals were favourite subjects of study. Mughal painting as a social art is quite at par with the other schools of Indian art, like Ajanta, Rajasthani, and Pahari paintings.

The Mughal school is not a reflection of the past and its rise can be traced to the changing reality, noteworthy in the history of world art. With the Mughal school the spiritual and the transcendental were not the leitmotif, in contrast to classical Indian art where painting focused primarily on religious themes and their purpose was religious propagation. New themes of painting other than the religious emerged in fifteenth-century Malwa paintings (Mandu school), and the illustrations of the manuscripts *Nimatnama* (Cookery Book) and *Miftah-ul Fuzala* (A Persian Lexicon) led to a fresh conceptual and stylistic expression in art. Akbar (r. 1556–1605) gave a new direction to painting by encouraging Islamic, Indian, and European themes, besides religious themes, accommodating historical and non-historical subjects. This enlarged scope of painting benefited the artists' vocabulary of icons, symbols, and signs, which conditioned their art to a great extent. The choice of themes for the paintings executed at Akbar's atelier was also influenced by his liberal and tolerant attitude towards all religions, especially Hinduism and Christianity. A number of Hindu epics, such as the *Harivansha*, the *Mahabharata*, and the *Ramayana*, were translated into Persian, and these were often illustrated with pictures. Abbreviated Persian translations of Indian classical works seem to have been aimed at making Akbar's courtiers conversant with Indian cultural values. Akbar is reported to have asked his nobles to acquire copies of the *Razmnama* (Persian translation of the *Mahabharata*), decorated with pictures. Similarly, the *Dastan-i Masih* (Life of Christ) was illustrated at Akbar's atelier, in addition to the numerous copies of European paintings and engravings depicting Christian themes, most notably by the artist Kesavdas. The *Dastan-i Masih* or *Miratul Quds* (The Mirror of Holiness), a Persian translation of a work in Portuguese based on the Gospels, was executed in 1602 on Akbar's orders by Father Jerome Xavier in collaboration with Maulana Abdus Sattar bin Qasim Lahori.

Babur (r. 1526–30), the first ruler of the Mughal dynasty, though a great lover of nature and with the vision of an art critic, is not known to have employed painters. As a critic, he comments on the celebrated Persian master painter Bihzad that 'his work was very dainty but he did not draw beardless faces well; he used greatly to lengthen the double chin (*ghab ghab*); bearded faces he drew admirably' (1530). He also mentions another famous Persian painter, Shah Muzaffar, and writes that 'he painted dainty portraits, representing the hair very daintily'. Babur had illustrated manuscripts in his royal library, demonstrating his interest in painting. The illustrated copies of the *Shahnama* (Timurid school, c. 1440) and the *Zafarnama* of 1467, containing Bihzad's painting, were in Babur's collection. However, there is no evidence of painters and painting at his court in India although his son, Mirza Kamran, possibly had the painters working for him. An illustrated manuscript, *Yusuf wa Zulaykha* of Jami (illustrated with six miniatures in the Bukhara style c. 1550–70), is said to have been copied for Kamran, in all likelihood at Kabul. However, the miniatures do not necessarily seem contemporary with the manuscript (c. 1530–40). The famous Persian master painter Maulana Dost Musauwir is believed to have worked for Mirza Kamran for a short period of time.

There is no painting extant executed under Mughal patronage prior to AH 956/1549–50, the year when Mir Sayyid Ali and Khwaja Abdu-s Samad joined Humayun's court at Kabul. However, an incident recorded in the *Tazkereh al Vakiat* indicates that in 1542, when Humayun was in Amarkot on his way to Persia, he had painters accompanying his retinue:

> Soon after the Rana retired, the king undressed, and ordered his clothes to be washed, and in the meanwhile he wore his dressing gown; while thus sitting, a beautiful bird flew into the tent, the doors of which were immediately shut, and the bird caught; His Majesty then took a pair of scissors and cut some of the feathers of the animal; he then sent for a painter,

and had taken a picture of the bird, and afterwards ordered it to be released.

Bayazid Bayat offers an interesting account of the painters at Humayun's court during the later years of his life at Kabul and Delhi. He writes that amongst the officials who accompanied Humayun from Kabul to Delhi in 1555 was one Hashim Haini, *Darogha-i Kitabkhana* (Superintendent of the Royal Library). In the same list one finds names of the following Persian painters: Mir Sayyid Ali, Khwaja Abdu-s Samad, Dost Musauwir, and Maulana Yusuf. Though the last two painters at the Mughal atelier did not execute any painting, their influence on the paintings under Humayun and Akbar cannot be ruled out.

The earliest painting executed at Kabul was probably the miniature in the *Muraqqa'-i Gulshan*, Gulistan Palace Library, Tehran: 'Two youths sitting in a landscape, one painting (probably Akbar), the other playing *rubab*—a stringed instrument' (upper part of the folio) by Abdu-s Samad. An inscription on it reads: *'Amal-i Nau-rozi Maulana Abdu-s Samad dar nimroz sakhta, san 958* (Work [done] on Nav-roz [the Persian New Year's Day] by Maulana Abdu-s Samad, made in half a day, AH 958/1551). The style of the miniature is Persian, the only non-Persian influence being Akbar's turban, which reflects the fashion of Humayun's court. Another album page, 'Humayun, his brothers and royal ladies in a garden', is almost contemporaneous with it. Although its overall style strongly suggests the Safavid style of the Tabriz school, it is attributed to Dost Muhammad of Shah Tahmasp's court, identified with the Dost Muhammad of Bayazid Bayat.

Another work, 'Emperors and princes of the House of Timur' (BM), probably executed at Kabul, is a large painting (executed on cloth measuring 108.5 cm × 108 cm) depicting Humayun's court (c. 1552–4). It represented the work of the Safavid artists. During Jahangir's reign this painting was retouched and overpainted. A recent finding of Francis Richard of a manuscript of the *Khamsa* of Nizami, in the Kasturbhai Collection, Ahmedabad, datable 1550–4, further enriches the wealth of paintings known to have been executed under Humayun at Kabul. Its illustrations, bereft of Indian elements, exhibit an amalgam of Tabrizi and Bukharan elements. It contains 34 miniatures of which 17 are distinctly Persian (11 in Bukharan style, 6 are affiliated with the Safavid style of Tabriz), and the remaining betray a mixture of Indian and Persian styles. Of course, these illustrations have no uniformity of style, and in them varying trends influencing the early Mughal painters' work are visible.

The development of Mughal painting can be entirely attributed to Akbar's characteristic enthusiasm and love for the art from childhood. Akbar took great interest in painting and to extend his support to it, he had the prices of art materials carefully assessed, and then devised a smooth process for obtaining the necessary materials. Akbar made it a point to personally examine the painters' work critically and confer rewards in order to encourage them.

In addition, for the first time, a conscious effort was made under Akbar to liberate painting from sectarian ideology, in contrast to traditional Indian art, including the Rajput school, which intensely focused on religious themes. As a Muslim, he marshalled a subtle philosophical argument against the Islamic theological disapproval of painting. He believed that a painter had quite peculiar means of recognizing God; for a painter in sketching anything that has life he only copies from something created by God and feels that he cannot bestow any individuality upon his work. The painter is thus forced to think of God, the giver of life. By this claim Akbar empowered painting as a source of revelation of divine wisdom.

This implies disagreement with the traditions of Prophet Mohammad, which forbids representation of living creatures, or acquiring or looking at them. It also contests the charge of blasphemy against the practitioners of the art of painting. Nevertheless, Akbar's appreciation of the art of painting could never fully counter the centuries-old Islamic condemnation of painting.

Mughal paintings, freed from religious association, renounced iconic and symbolic representation in favour of non-symbolic and descriptive visual documents of contemporary life. While depicting themes related to the legends and myths of Islam (for example, in the illustrations of the *Hamzanama*), the artists' visual narratives are simply interpretative and their choice of subject matter to represent the theme is only functional. Similarly, in the treatment of themes illustrating great Hindu epics like the *Ramayana* and the *Harivansha*, the Mughal artists' approach to the subject matter is purely documentary. Their descriptive visual narratives do not intend to arouse any religious sentiment. In general, the Mughal school of the sixteenth century never intended to project ideology or philosophy of any sect, cult, or faith. This made Mughal painting completely secular.

Like Akbar, Jahangir also took personal interest in the work of his painters. By looking at the miniature paintings executed by a variety of artists, Jahangir acquired an intimate knowledge of their individual styles and could recognize their work without the artist's name being revealed to him. Jahangir, a generous patron of artists and an enthusiastic connoisseur of painting, was proud of his painters and their work, and believed them to be quite at par with their European contemporaries.

Jahangir considered painting to be a form of historical documentation of the wonders of nature and the peculiar and unusual events in everyday life. Such pictures naturally aroused the curiosity, amazement, and pleasure of onlookers. Jahangir's unceasing passion for exotic nature and wildlife prompted a new subject of painting, that is, pictures on natural history. The portrayal of the strange and unfamiliar never ceased to fascinate him. Also, accuracy in the depiction of the details of an object was strictly formalized under the rigour of Jahangir's keen eye. Jahangir craved for detailed and, hence, truthful graphic description of an object, and pictorial narratives with physical reality became the mainstay of painters.

Jahangir, like his father, had portraits painted of his nobles, which were collected together in albums. He had portraits painted of the nobles of the Mughal court as well as of Safavid and Uzbek rulers, princes, and nobles. He sent his painter Bishandas to Iran especially to prepare portraits of the ruler, Shah 'Abbas I, and his nobles. A few portraits of Shah 'Abbas and his courtiers, done by Bishandas in Iran (1613–19), are thus a result of the artist's direct observation. Jahangir was so pleased with Bishandas's achievement that in 1619 he presented him with an elephant, which was a status symbol in Mughal India. He also checked the authenticity of the portraits with those who had seen the person concerned.

His interest in exactitude gave further impetus to the production of historical portraits with an unexpectedly intimate and personal character, for which the Mughal school is famous. Vincent Smith (1911) observes that the works of the Indo-Persian draughtsmen and painters furnish a gallery of historical portraits, lifelike and perfectly authentic, that enables historians to know the personal appearance of all the Mughal emperors and many other prominent personalities of the era. It is doubtful if any other country in the world possesses a better series of portraits of men who made history.

Under Shah Jahan (r. 1628–58), portraiture still held pride of place. The likenesses of the emperor and the nobles continued to be the key focus of portrait painting. Apotheosis portrait of the emperor, as well as genealogical and equestrian portraits, were the subjects of the artists' attention. In a genealogical painting there is an imaginary setting in which three emperors, Akbar, Jahangir, and Shah Jahan, in a group emerged as a typified composition. The portrayal of ascetics and saints was another area of artistic interest.

Paintings executed during the reign of Shah Jahan, although accommodating earlier Mughal trends in aesthetics, showed an explicit emphasis on idealization imbued with dazzling ornamentation, decorative surface, and superbly detailed descriptions. This obscured the humanistic elements such as the penetrating psychological insight and exceptional naturalism that were evident during Jahangir's period. Shah Jahan's innate love for surface brilliance and ornate objects drew an artist's work very close to the accomplishment of a skilled draftsman. His great fondness for jewellery and architecture richly inlaid with precious stones (*parchinkari*) left an impact on the paintings of his reign. These exhibit an abundant use of gold, glimmering jewels, richly woven textile, and profuse surface decoration on architectural columns, which went much against the characteristics of the art of Jahangir's atelier that reflected physical reality, harmonious colour effects, and naturalism. Nonetheless, the portrayal of ordinary men continued to reveal naturalistic trends even during Shah Jahan's reign. In such paintings the lifelike rendering of human figures, the chiaroscuro effect, and the treatment of space reveals an in-depth understanding of the European perspective and the humanist element of Mughal art. Otherwise, in general, Shah Jahan's period represents the most luxuriant phase of Mughal painting in terms of richness of ornamentation and technical perfection. It was a reinterpretation of the Mughal style, largely conditioned by Shah Jahan's passion for visual splendour, idealized or perfected images, and admirably detailed surface descriptions. This departure in the Mughal style from naturalism to an idealized reality tended to encourage pseudo-realism in art. In Shah Jahani portraits an individual is defined in terms of externals bereft of psychological insight. Obviously, Shah Jahan's penchant for perfect idealism took the edge off the Jahangiri humanistic vision in art and led to a change in Mughal taste and aesthetics. The glorious chapter of the Mughal painting was, however, abruptly and unexpectedly cut short by Aurangzeb's (r. 1658–1707) indifference to the art of painting.

Mughal patrons always gave recognition to an artist's achievement and honoured them with lofty titles. Humayun conferred upon Mir Sayyid Ali and Khwaja Abdu-s Samad the titles *Nadir-ul Mulk* and *Shirin Qalam* (literally, Sweet Pen), respectively. Basawan, La'l, Mansur, and Miskin of Akbar's atelier had the honorific title of *Ustad* (Master). Jahangir honoured Abu'l Hasan and Ustad Mansur with the titles *Nadir-uz Zaman* (Wonder of the Age) and *Nadir-ul Asr* (Unique of the Age), respectively. A patron's generosity was expressed in several other ways. Bishandas, sent to Persia to execute portraits of Shah 'Abbas I and his courtiers, was honoured by Jahangir with the gift of an elephant upon his return in recognition of his mastery of portrait painting.

Jahangir also appreciated the merit of a painting by commenting on the painting and providing his signature to it. Such ascriptions, appearing on numerous paintings, bear testimony to his judgement. These observations are invaluable records of his status as a connoisseur. On a miniature, 'A prince giving wine to a young beautiful woman' (WAG, W.668) by Abu'l Hasan, Jahangir writes: *Kar-i khub-i Nadir-uz Zaman* (A good piece of work by Nadir–uz Zaman, that is, Abu'l Hasan). A similar comment appears alongside his autograph on the portrait of Sultan Muhammad Qutbu-l Mulk (VA, IM, 22–1925), executed by Hashim (see Figure 1). It reads: *Shabih-i khub Sultan Muhammad Qutbu-l Mulk* (A good likeness of Sultan Muhammad Qutbu-l Mulk). Hashim must have excelled in portraits, since on another portrait drawn by him (MMA, 55.121.10.33) Jahangir's appraisal is the same: *Shabih-i khub Ibrahim Adil Khan* (A good likeness of Ibrahim Adil Khan).

Shah Jahan, too, like his predecessors, never fell short in his appreciation of paintings. On a portrait of him (VA, IM, 17–1925), he writes: *Shabih-i khub, chihlsalagi-i man ast, 'amal-i Bichitr* (A good portrait of me in my 40th year, the work of Bichitr) (see Figure 2). Such

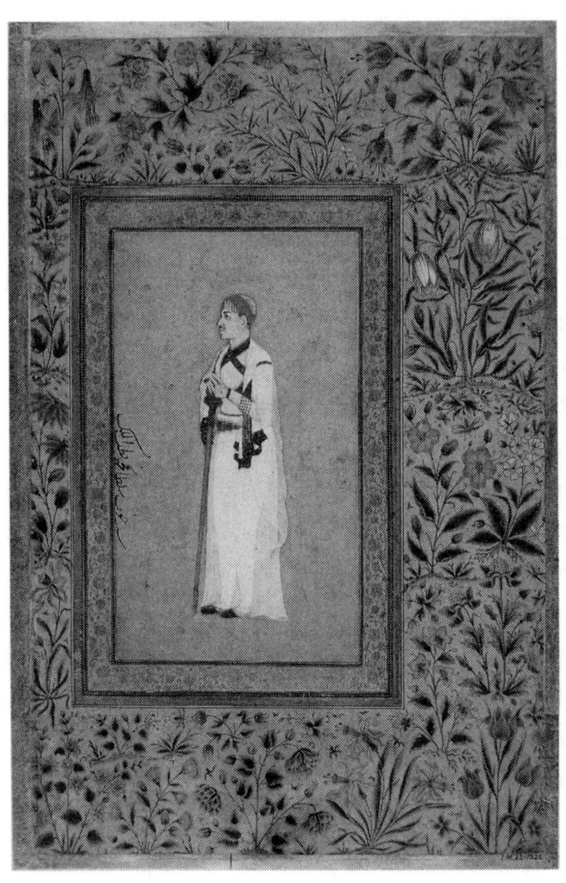

FIGURE 1 Sultan Muhammad Qutub Shah of Golconda. By Hashim, c. 1624–5. Minto Album, Victoria and Albert Museum, London (IM, 22-1925).

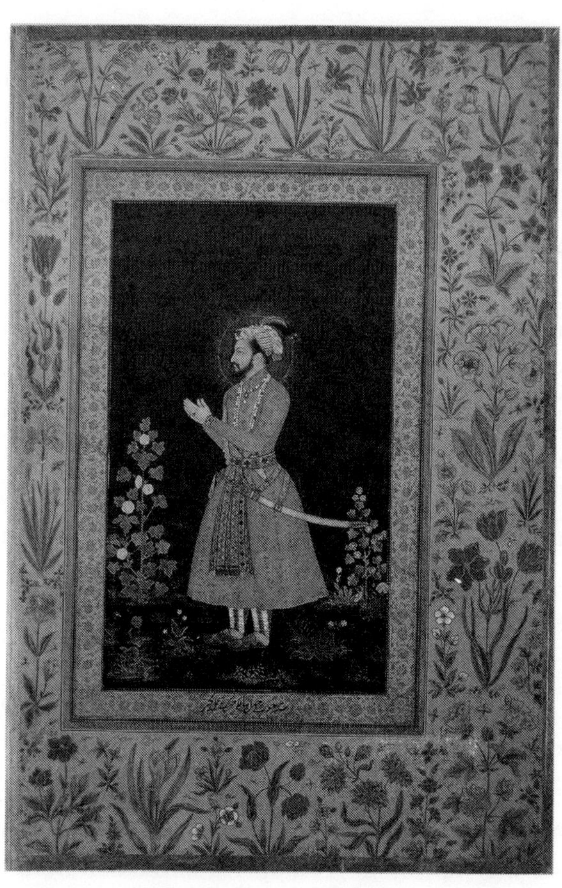

FIGURE 2 Shah Jahan with hands lifted in prayer. By Bichitr, c. 1631. Minto Album, Victoria and Albert Museum, London (IM, 17–1925).

autographed notes of the patrons not only acknowledged a painter's excellence, but also established him as a skilled artist. Besides, the emperors' autographs hint at their personal rapport with the painters and their work. These are also a testimony to the Mughal emperors' love of painting.

Mughal patrons liked to have the painters accompany them during excursions, expeditions, and other ventures. Jahangir has noted in his memoirs that Mansur painted the flowers of the Kashmir valley during his own sojourn in Kashmir in 1620 and among the events of that year, he notes that Mansur drew the likeness of the bird *saj* (dipper) seen at Sukh Nag in the Kashmir valley. A record of such events clearly shows that the painters accompanied the royal camp whenever the emperor moved out of the capital.

Artist's movement away from the atelier must have been common as, to draw the likeness of individuals, they must have had to visit their subjects. They drew paintings of birds, animals, flowers, and plants, and the like, after careful observation. An illustration from the *Masnavi* (1663) of Zafar Khan (RAS, MS. Pers. 310, folios 19b–20a)—'An artist taking portraits of the individuals in the assembly of poets and scholars'—

supports the view that portraits were executed on the spot, outside the studio.

During the medieval period the art of painting was often hereditary. The contemporary Persian chronicles and the ascriptions on the paintings offer ample information on such hereditary succession. Mir Sayyid Ali, a Persian master painter at Humayun's and Akbar's courts, under whose supervision the first four volumes of the *Hamzanama* were completed, was the illustrious son of Mir Mansur (or Musauwir), an artist of the Tabriz school. Muhammad Sharif, son of another famous Persian master painter, Khwaja Abdu-s Samad, was also a painter. The illustrated manuscripts *Khamsa* of Nizami (BM, Or. 12208) and *Razmnama* (SMS) were prepared under the supervision of Muhammad Sharif. *Razmnama* also contains miniatures executed by Muhammad Sharif. Aqa Riza of Herat, a painter at Prince Salim's studio and later at Jahangir's court, had two sons, Abu'l Hasan and Abid, both of whom were actively engaged in painting till Shah Jahan's time. Jahangir, who honoured Abu'l Hasan with the title *Nadir-uz Zaman* (Wonder of the Age), writes that in the art of painting, he excelled his father: 'There is, however, no comparison between his work and that of his father [i.e. he is far superior to the latter]. One cannot put them into the same category.' In another instance, Manohar, the son of Basawan, a prolific painter of Akbar's court, had a long, active career as an artist. Bishandas, known for portrait painting at Jahangir's studio, was the nephew of Nanha, a painter active at Akbar's and Jahangir's courts. Among other instances, we know of the artists Mukhlis and his son Ali, and Nand and his son Ramdas, both active at Akbar's atelier. Likewise, two brothers Asi and Miskin are well known for their paintings in the *Akbarnama* at Victoria & Albert Museum, London. Nevertheless, the information available to us is meagre. The continuity of the tradition of painting can be explained to an extent by its hereditary character and this is also true of the other art forms in India.

In the Islamic tradition an artist sometimes simultaneously practised both calligraphy and painting (miniature and mural). Khwaja Abdu-s Samad, a native of Shiraz, was a 'painter-scribe'. Humayun recognized his skill as a calligraphist and bestowed upon him the title *Shirin Qalam*. In some of the ascriptions (including the artist's signature) on the miniatures, his name appears with the suffix 'Shirin Qalam'. Abdu-s

Samad also executed murals and this is evident from the account of an event that took place during a feast at Aziz Koka's palace. Farid Bhakkari writes in his *Zakhiratu'l Khwanin* that Aziz Koka told Muhammad Sharif: 'Nawab [Muhammad Sharif], you are not kind to me; but what love your late father Mulla Abdu-s Samad Musauwir [Painter] showed me! Why, all the pictures and paintings that you see in this private chamber [*khilwat-khana*] were made by his august hand.'

A rare piece of information available on the painter Daswant would probably suggest that in India too a painter could practise both miniature and mural painting. About Daswant, Abu'l Fazl writes that he devoted his entire life to art and even painted figures on walls.

In medieval times, painting as a profession appears to have been a male domain, as only a few women painters are known to have worked at the Mughal atelier. The ascriptions given on the Mughal miniatures reveal their names, namely Nadira Banu, daughter of Mir Taqi and pupil of Aqa Riza (the well-known painter in the service of Prince Salim during Akbar's reign); Ruqaiya Banu; and Sahifa Banu. No further information is available about them. However, the style of their work establishes their affiliation with Jahangir's studio.

Amongst the large number of the painters of the Mughal school, the total number of Muslim painters is less than that of the Hindu painters. As many as 201 of 327 Mughal painters were Hindus (to judge from their names), while the remaining 126 were Muslims, several of whom must have been converts or descendants of converted Hindus, as the number of Muslim immigrants into India was insignificant during the sixteenth and seventeenth centuries. However, it is not always possible to separate the immigrants from the converts; some of the Muslim painters retained their designations that betrayed their Hindu origin.

The artist at the Mughal court was given recognition as an individual. This was in contrast to the traditional art centres like those of Ajanta, eastern India, and western India, where the artist as an individual was hardly known and thus his specific contribution as an individual remains unidentified. In Indian art, ascribed miniatures are known only from the sixteenth century onwards, the earliest examples being the works from Akbar's atelier. However, at Akbar's atelier, too, the earliest known works, namely the illustrations of the *Hamzanama* (c. 1565–80), *Anwar-i Suhaili* (dated 1570), and *Tutinama* (c. 1565–70), are anonymous. The works executed after 1582 are mostly ascribed. This practice made it possible to recognize an artist as an individual and assess his personal achievements. Thus, each individual artist had the opportunity to display his characteristic originality, making him conscious of his individuality. Thus, the ground was prepared for ushering individualism into their art.

Genesis of the Mughal School

Early Mughal paintings show a mix of different art traditions and can be divided into two categories: (*a*) those inspired by western India or Gujarati style (the *Chaurapanchasika* and the *Chandayana* styles); and (*b*) those showing affinity to the school of Persia, and sometimes directly derived from Tabriz, Shiraz, Bukhara, and Herat schools. This categorization is based on predominant features of particular styles exhibited in the miniatures, although, in general, there appears a mingling of various art forms even in a single piece. Nevertheless, this amalgamation of different art traditions is not found in a coherent manner in any particular manuscript, and, therefore, an impression of the smooth emergence of a definite style is lacking. However, this phenomenon did not come to an end even after the Mughal style was fully established and had reached its zenith. A possible reason was the employment of painters of different origins in the Mughal atelier at varying stages of its growth and development.

In the early illustrations of the *Hamzanama*, the compositions are simple and often intended to be symmetrical. In them, restricted movement, similar to the Safavid school, is evident but lacks its fineness of lines. Besides, flat depiction of architectural columns with profuse surface embellishment in a jewel-like manner and the use of a limited palette of bright colours strictly follow Persian conventions and show affinity to the Safavid school. Here the function of the colour is purely decorative as are the drawings comprising geometrical patterns and arabesques. The signs of naturalism and rhythm in the rendering of forms, treatment of space with the introduction of subsidiary scenes set against the background, and trees with dense foliage and brilliant blossoms seen in the later *Hamzanama* paintings are manifestations of Indian traditions. The paintings thus combined the qualities of a number of different schools. In this context, an observation of D. Barrett and B. Gray (1963) on a miniature, 'Mihrdukht shoots her bow at the ring' (c. 1570), is relevant: The action takes place in a walled garden in which Mihrdukht is impetuously shooting at the bird surmounting the many-staged minaret on the upper story of a pavilion. The luxuriant trees of the garden and still more the exotic plants scattered below them remind one of the paintings of the school of Deccan. The girls in the pavilion wear transparent muslin veil (*orhni*) and show the energetic movement of the earliest known Rajasthani miniatures, while behind the group on the upper floor is a dark-complexioned girl, directly inspired by a Tanjore wall painting. In fact, everything points to the painter having been trained in the Deccan school. Of course, the design and layout of the page conform to the Mughal conception. The *Hamzanama* illustrations, datable to 1562–80, display a range of artistic trends and methods of rendering figures and other objects. These trends provide definite clues to the different art traditions that played a role in the formation of the Mughal school. However, these appear out of sequence. Broadly, there was a clear shift away from the Persian conventions, and an effort to achieve a three-dimensional effect coupled with more vivid range of colours was clearly evident (see Figure 3).

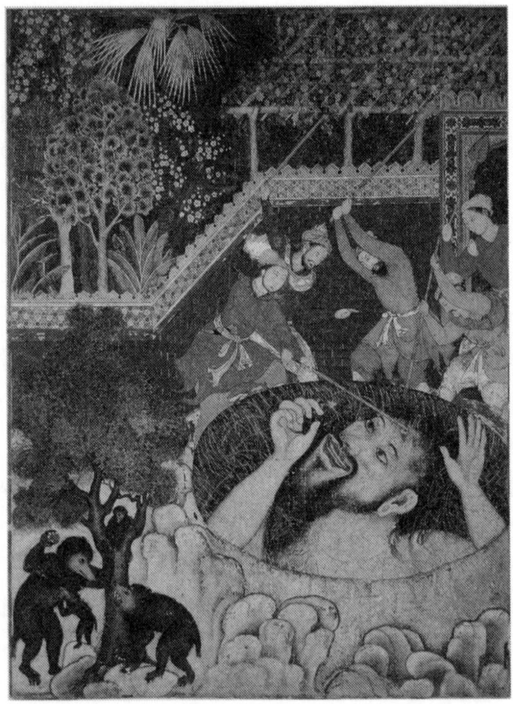

FIGURE 3 Gardeners beating the giant Zumurrod Shah, who is trapped in a well. Tempera on cotton. Illustration to the *Hamzanama*, c. 1562–77. Victoria and Albert Museum, London (IS 1516-1883).

It is notable that the *Hamzanama* paintings are in style closer to the Indian tradition than the Persian. Here, the characteristic treatment of the picture space, with an arrangement of plane behind plane, or subsidiary scenes set in the background, is fundamentally Indian and not Persian. In the numerous folios of the *Hamzanama*, the treatment of trees is in the characteristic Indian style with foliage painted against a dark background. Moreover, the luxuriant depiction of foliage and the brilliant blossoms in the *Hamzanama* are derivations from Deccan paintings. It should be noted, however, that the extraordinary vigour of action and violent movement seen in several illustrations of the *Hamzanama* is altogether absent in the pre-Mughal art of the book in India and also in the art of Persia. It was a new element that brought originality to the Mughal painter's work and marked the emergence of a new style, that is, the Mughal. The Safavid (Tabriz school) tradition never throve in India in its purest form; and the early Mughal paintings exhibited Indian traditions, particularly the vigorous realism of the Rajasthani school.

The marked shift from exact adherence to the Persian convention is visible even in some of the works executed during Humayun's reign. The naturalism and the interaction of figures in the miniature 'Princes of the House of Timur' (c. 1550–5) and in several other miniatures of the *Khamsa* of Nizami (c. 1550–5) in the Lalbhai Collection, Ahmedabad, is explicit. These miniatures clearly differ from the more stylized compositions of the Safavid school. In fact, this shift reveals a coherent, consistent, and dynamic mode of expression. In general, in fifteenth-to-sixteenth-century Persian art, the trend of breaking up a scene into two or more groups/units was in vogue, but these units remained isolated in the absence of any attempt on the part of the artist to show some kind of a relationship between them. The Mughal artists did succeed in connecting the units through rhythmic movements, gestures, and facial expressions. In their work there appeared something free, bold, and with a more vigorous effect than that ever expressed by Persian painters. The vitality and the inner coherence and unity of the *Hamzanama* illustrations cannot be explained by the Persian sources alone. The indigenous elements also contributed greatly to the development of the Mughal style.

Traditions of Bukhara art, too, crept into the Mughal school at its formative stage, a striking example of which is a miniature in the *Anwar-i Suhaili* (dated 1570, SOAS) of Mughal provenance. This particular miniature, 'A monkey caught in a carpenter's wedge', which appears on folio 40, is an unsigned work. This miniature, characteristically of flat pure colours with a preference for gold to depict the sky, simplified character of the picture both in terms of the number of figures and also in the range of colours, richness in the intensity of colour, and decorative colouring rather than naturalistic colouring in the picture, is close to the Bukhara tradition. Besides, the undulated mounds of earth defining the horizon, a stream in the foreground with its edges strewn with stones, and the flowering plants in the foreground further affiliate its style with the Persian conventions adapted in the Bukhara style. Quite a few of the miniatures of this manuscript are by an artist trained in the Bukhara style who had not yet adjusted his style to the Akbari synthesis.

In another instance, two miniatures of the manuscript *Duval Rani Khizr Khan* (dated 1567, NM, No. L.53-2/7) clearly show the impact of the Bukhara tradition on the early Mughal style. These two miniatures, (*a*) 'Old wrestler defeats his arrogant pupil' and (*b*) 'A fiery horse brought before Prince Khizr Khan', are close to the Bukhara-influenced paintings of the *Gulistan* of Sa'di, datable c. 1567–8 (BM, Or. 5302). In these paintings, the presentation of an arabesque pattern decorating the throne, carpet, and so on; the facial features of the prince, attendants, and wrestlers; the use of flat pure colours; and the sky depicted in gold are identifiable with the Bukhara school. Nevertheless, the rhythmic folds in the costumes with shaded lines and casual shading in the architectural columns, the variety of gestures depicted in relation to the human figures, and the action-filled figures of the violent horse and the vigilant groom also draw them close to the indigenous traditions. It is a good example of an amalgam of a range of different traditions taking place at the royal atelier from the very outset, that is, 1568. The *Duval Rani Khizr Khan* is the earliest dated illustrated manuscript of the Mughal school. Its miniatures bear a similarity to Bukharan prototypes and are characteristic of the *Hamza* style. It should be noted that all the three manuscripts, *Gulistan*, *Duval Rani Khizr Khan*, and *Anwar-i Suhaili*, demonstrate a close affinity to the *Hamzanama* style in the details of human figures, landscape, and architecture. In these manuscripts the human figures appear imbued with spirited action that is in contrast to the Persian tradition, in which they appear isolated in composition and their action is subdued. By 1567–70 the identifiable style of the *Hamzanama* illustrations marked the beginning of the Mughal school.

The miniatures of *Anwar-i Suhaili* show an improvement in the treatment of space, marked by an openness in the composition. There is sufficient room left for the main action, thus bringing the central theme into focus with clarity. In the outdoor scenes, the hillocks, streams, plants, and trees, while accentuating the effect of depth and distance in the picture, add to the drama and lend the scene a sense of liveliness. Here the artist hints at receding effects in landscape, which is not evident in the miniatures of *Duval Rani Khizr Khan* and *Gulistan*. The most significant change evident in the miniatures of *Anwar-i Suhaili*, virtually absent in the above two manuscripts, is naturalism, an element wanting in Persian art. Objects represented in the Persian paintings are purely linear and decorative. Their forms appear conventional and stylized, and lacking relief-effect. An attempt at modelling with deep-shaded strokes in the depiction of costumes and architectural columns is another feature that separates the illustrations of *Anwar-i Suhaili* from the linear art of Persia. In the *Anwar-i Suhaili,* in contrast to *Hamzanama* paintings, there is also a refinement in the lines and an improvement in the colour-palette. The brilliant colour effect of many of the paintings of the *Hamzanama* is missing in the miniatures of the *Anwar-i Suhaili* where the pigments are in graded tones. These are strong in effect but never glaring and bright. This improvement in the artist's palette gave rise to naturalism in art and a concentration on the action of the figures to establish a rhythm. It further emphasized naturalism. The psychological relationship between the figures is in contrast to the almost entirely formal relation depicted in the Persian style. This approach of the Mughal artist drew his art closer to reality. The Mughal painter's approach to the depiction of animals is also close to the Indian tradition. An Indian element, that is, sympathy with the animal world, gave rise to emotions and feelings in their representation.

A significant characteristic of the depiction of birds and animals in the Mughal style was realism, apparent from the very outset in the Mughal painters' work. This trend goes much against the idealized representation of animals common in Persian tradition. Thus, in the miniatures of *Anwar-i Suhaili*, the depiction of animals is more natural than the remote and exquisite animals of the Persian school. They are more deeply engaged in action and much realism is achieved in their images through shading and modelling. This emphasis on naturalism, an approach credited to the Indian style, makes the Mughal painter someone exploring the objective characteristics of the natural world.

The miniatures of the *Tutinama*, datable 1570–5, are even more important as these broadly represent a summing up of pre-Mughal Indian art, encompassing sundry traits of the fifteenth-to-sixteenth-century Indian centres of Islamic painting and regional styles observed in the manuscripts *Chaurapanchasika* and *Chandayana* (both derived from the fifteenth-century western India school). The amalgam of various traditions of art in this manuscript poses the problem of tracing the original traditions of the painters who executed its illustrations. The 'fish-eyed' figure of women in the *Tutinama*, emerged from the chaurapanchasika style, is seen in this manuscript to a greater degree in the depiction of females rather than males. This is reflected in the women's long eyes, broad cheeks, heavy breasts, and costumes (patterned with rosettes, chequers, and stars) with triangular ends, and earrings (peg-shaped and rosette-shaped). The characteristic depiction of females with one breast overlapping with the other on several folios of the *Tutinama* is akin to the Malwa tradition (the centre of the western India school at Mandu). This peculiar style is well represented in the *Kalpasutra*, illustrated at Mandu (NM, MS 49. 175). Also, traces of the Deccan art (Golconda) are visible in some of the miniatures of this manuscript, for example, in the treatment of grass, trees, and streams.

The most notable aspect of *Tutinama* miniatures is the lively effect achieved in the depiction of figures, where the emphasis is on establishing a psychological relationship between them, resulting in the figures having a very animated look. This naturalistic and expressive quality of art was a major feature of the Mughal style. Deep shading and bold strokes in the treatment of figures and landscape was an improvement over the two-dimensional pictures from Persia and western India/Gujarati school. These striking features were derived from Renaissance art in the 1570s at the

Mughal atelier which show signs of the emergence of a unique and composite style.

Rounded hillocks with 'comma-like' strokes, tufts of grass, and clouds with rosette- and ribbon–like folds, seen on the several folios of the *Tutinama*, seem to have been directly derived from the Safavid tradition. Besides, the treatment of human figures, trees, and landscape in the *Tutinama* is akin to the style of the *Hamzanama* paintings. Similarities found in their representation show a close relationship in style between a group of the *Tutinama* illustrations and the *Hamzanama* paintings.

However, there is a lack of unity in the illustrations of the *Hamzanama*, *Tutinama*, and *Anwar-i Suhaili*. One encounters different indigenous styles and characteristics of various centres of Persian painting. Numerous illustrations of the *Hamzanama* show more unity of style as compared to the other two works. The reason for this might be the completion date, that is, 1580. By this time different traditions of art had been absorbed or reconciled with the Mughal artists' work. Consequently, there emerged a common style of rendering forms, handling space, and colour schemes. Could it be suggested then that the genesis of the Mughal style lies in the adoption of different traditions?

In the context of the European traditions, the deep shading and heavy modelling seen in the treatment of costumes in the *Tutinama* illustrations and the depiction of perspective by the representation of distant objects in the *Hamzanama* (but without understanding the result of visual effects in relation to the gradual increase of distance) are willingly followed in the later illustrations of the *Razmnama* (SMS, c. 1584), *Ta'rikh-i Khandan-i Timuria* (OPL, c. 1585), *Ramayana* (SMS, AD 1587), and *Darabnama* (BM, c. 1585–90). This reinforces the fact that the trends that existed during the formation of style survived, albeit with greater clarity and understanding.

Moreover, even the art of the master Mughal artists, who had established themselves in the tradition of Persian painting, got eclipsed at Akbar's atelier, where both indigenous and foreign elements of art intermingled. Khwaja Abdu-s Samad, who joined Humayun's service at Kabul in 1549–50 and is recognized as one of the founders of the Mughal school, showed a strong affinity with the fifteenth-to-sixteenth-century Tabriz school. His style, at least till 1555, was fundamentally inspired by the Safavid style, derived from the works of the master Persian painter Bihzad. However, in his miniatures belonging to Akbar's reign, one can see many of the characteristic features of the early Mughal school. His miniature 'Khusrau hunting with dogs and cheetah' (c. 1595–6) reveals Indian 'realism' and 'spirited composition'. In this painting, the indications of European influence are of special interest, as these were absent in the artist's earlier works. This particular painting shows modelling with thin shading in the treatment of hills and animal drawings and blurred depiction of trees on the horizon.

Mir Sayyid Ali, notably influenced by Bihzad and faithful to the Safavid canons of art, was another founder member of the Mughal school. His early work explicitly exhibits a strong affiliation with the classic tradition of the Tabriz school. However, his later work at Akbar's atelier is influenced by the Indian traditions, that is, the vigorous realism of the Rajasthani school.

The work of both these painters, Mir Sayyid Ali and Khwaja Abdu-s Samad, at least till 1555, is wholly conservative and alien to the aesthetic innovations brought about at Akbar's atelier. Their works are strongly marked by Persian aesthetic traits, and techniques of European art like methods of shading, modelling, and perspective are totally absent.

The work of Mir Musauwir and Maulana Yusuf, painters of the Mughal atelier, are unfortunately not available till date. However, Dost Muhammad and Maulana Dervesh Muhammad are known through the miniatures probably executed at Humayun's atelier and attributed to them by modern scholars. The former bears explicit affiliation with the Safavid school and the latter with the Uzbek tradition centred at Bukhara.

Finally, the shift from the strict Persian conventions seen in the works of Mir Sayyid Ali and Khwaja Abdu-s Samad probably marked the true beginning of the Mughal school of painting. The realism of the Mughal school lies in the integration of the traditions imbibed from Iranian, Indian, and European centres of painting.

1

The Atelier

In ancient India, painters and paintings flourished under the rulers' patronage. Kalidas, Bana Bhatt, and Dandin refer to 'picture houses' (*chitrashalas*), paintings, and painters. The painters were employed by the royal establishment and instructed to paint according to royal tastes. There were also picture houses that were both royal and private. The rulers of the dynasties of eastern India, like the Somavansis and Gangas of Orissa, the Chandras, the Bahuma-Palas, as well as those in Assam, had their own artists. The ruling dynasties of central India, that is, the Parmaras and Chandellas, even had sculptors who worked for them. No specific evidence is, however, available relating to the establishment of an atelier under a ruler where several artists from diverse places worked under a single roof. In all likelihood, painters and sculptors were commissioned to work but they were not organized in a group working on a regular basis as a part of the royal establishment like the Mughal atelier (*tasvirkhana*). It is relevant to note that in the context of the celebration of the marriage of Harsha's daughter, Bana Bhatt writes that from every country skilled artists were summoned and a group of skilled painters painted auspicious scenes.

The active period of the Mughal school was between 1551 and 1658 and reached its zenith during the period 1610–27. Mughal paintings exhibit an eclectic art that was the result of works by painters from different lands and belonging to different traditions of painting, namely the Safavid and Timurid centres in Iran, Samarqand (Central Asia), Kabul, Bukhara, Kashmir (northern Indian subcontinent), Gujarat (western India), and lastly Bijapur and Golconda (southern India).

The atelier provided an opportunity for the artists to work on a regular basis and also facilitated interaction between artists from diverse traditions. Besides, the less–skilled artists learnt and received instructions in painting from master painters. The Mughal painters did not confine themselves to their specific traits: they freely adapted and incorporated subjects, styles, and techniques of others into their work.

The names of the painters who worked for Humayun prior to his exile in Persia (1540) are not known. However, the existence of an atelier at his court may be inferred from Jauhar's account (1587), which mentions that even during the most difficult times (August–September 1542, at Amarkot) Humayun had painters in his retinue. Bayazid Biyat's account of painting and painters of Humayun's court furnishes ample evidence on the later years of Humayun's life at Kabul and Delhi. Amongst the officials who accompanied him from Kabul to Delhi in 1555, Hashim Haini, *Darogha-i Kitabkhana* (Superintendent of the Royal Library) is mentioned. In the same list we also find the names of famous painters such as Mir Sayyid Ali, Khwaja Abdu-s Samad, Maulana Dost Musauwir, and Maulana Yusuf. This shows that painters worked in Humayun's establishment at Kabul in 1554. We also know that Mir Sayyid Ali and Khwaja Abdu-s Samad had joined his service in 1549–50. Additional information is available in the *Tuzuk-i Jahangiri* (1624), where in the context of

Hemu's death after his defeat in the Battle of Panipat (5 November 1556) it is narrated:

> The king [Akbar] answered, 'I have cut him in pieces before this', and explained: 'One day, in Kabul, I was copying a picture in presence of Khwaja Abdu-s Samad *Shirin Qalam*, when a form appeared from my brush, the parts of which were separate and divided from each other. One of those near asked, "Whose picture is this?" It came to my tongue to say that it was the likeness of Hemu.'

Thus, Akbar, as a young prince, took interest in painting, and received instruction in painting at Kabul.

During the brief period of his reign (July 1555–January 1556), Humayun had his library in a building in the Old Fort, Delhi. The atelier, an integral part of the royal library under the Mughal establishment, could have been situated in the precincts of this particular building (known as Sher Mandal). However, no dated miniature belonging to this period of Humayun's reign is known.

The organization of the royal atelier received its particular structure under Akbar. Akbar shifted his court to Agra when he captured the city in 1558. It was here that the atelier was rejuvenated after the sudden death of Humayun and the period of turmoil till Akbar consolidated his power by 1562. Under Akbar's personal direction, manuscript painting emerged as the main activity at the Agra atelier. An illustrated copy of the *Anwar-i Suhaili* (SOAS, MS 10102) carries a pictorial colophon showing the date and place, that is, AH 978/AD 1570. The *Tutinama* manuscript (CMA), though does not bear a colophon, could have been taken up at Agra, as based on style it can be dated to 1570–5. The miniatures of the great *Hamzanama* project (c. 1562–80) also began to be painted in 1562, that is, at the Agra atelier.

The imperial atelier apparently shifted to Fatehpur Sikri when Akbar made that city his capital in 1573. Monserrate (1580–2) refers to the imperial workshop for painters in the following words:

> For this purpose he has built a workshop near the palace. Where also are studios and work-rooms for the finer and more reputable arts, such as painting, goldsmith-work, tapestry-making, carpet and curtain-making, and the manufacturing of arms. Hither he very frequently comes and relaxes his mind with watching at their work those who practise these arts.

Although the exact location of individual workshops at Fatehpur Sikri are yet to be identified, some of them were in cells adjacent to the emperor's palace. These were administered as a part of the emperor's extensive household.

The most important project of this workshop was the *Hamzanama,* completed in twelve volumes, each containing 100 illustrations. Early references to this work appear in the *Nafaisul Maasir* (1573) and *Ta'rikh-i Akbari* (1580).

The work, initially supervised by Mir Sayyid Ali, was completed under the supervision of Khwaja Abdu-s Samad. Mir Sayyid Ali left for a pilgrimage to Mecca when only four volumes with illustrations were complete. However, the date of this event is not known; he must have left prior to the date of compilation of the *Nafaisul Maasir,* that is, 1573. The *Nafaisul Maasir* records that Khwaja Abdu-s Samad succeeded him in this office. Abdu-s Samad lived at Fatehpur Sikri during this period. In 1578, he was appointed superintendent of the royal mint at Fatehpur Sikri and in 1583 he was given the additional charge of leather articles.

A copy of the illustrated manuscript *Gulistan* of Sa'di (RAS, MS 258), provided with a pictorial colophon, is significant. Its colophon bears the date 1581 and the place Fatehpur, showing that the imperial atelier was then active in that city.

As many manuscripts either lack colophons or omit the name of the place where they were completed, no other illustrated manuscript cites the name Fatehpur. However, the manuscripts known to have been illustrated during Akbar's stay at Fatehpur Sikri, up to May 1586, can safely be described as the production of the atelier at Fatehpur, notable among which are the *Razmnama* (SMS), c. 1584, and the *Ta'rikh-i Khandan-i Timuria* (OPL), c. 1584–6.

Once Fatehpur Sikri was abandoned as the capital, the atelier shifted to the new imperial seat, Lahore (1586–98). Here at least four manuscripts were prepared. These are the *Diwan* of Anwari (FAM), dated 1588; the *Baharistan* of Jami (BLO, Elliot MS 254), dated 1595; *Anwar-i Suhaili* (BKB), dated 1596–7; and the *Khamsa* of Amir Khusrau (WAG, W.624), dated 1597–8. Colophons in these manuscripts give the date as well as the location—as Lahore. Other manuscripts give dates but not the name of the city where these were illustrated, for example, *Ramayana* (SMS), dated 1587; the *Khamsa* of Nizami (BM, Or. 12208), dated

1596–7, and *Jami'ut Tawarikh* (IL), dated 1596. They must also have been illustrated at Lahore.

After 1598, till his death in 1605, Akbar had his capital at Agra where the manuscripts *Nufahat ul Uns* (BM, Or. 1362), dated 1602–3, and the *Bostan* of Sa'di (FAM), dated 1605, according to their colophons, were produced. It is notable that the atelier, as also the imperial library, moved from one city to another with the shifting of the capital.

Princes and nobles followed the example set by the emperor and art flourished at capital cities and regional centres in *suba*s (provinces). Jahangir was not only passionate about painting but also a connoisseur of art. He had maintained a busy studio and had painters at his establishment at Allahabad as a governor. The manuscripts *Diwan* of Amir Nizamuddin Hasan (WAG, W.650), dated 1602–3, and *Rajkunwar* (CBL), dated 1603–4, were completed at Allahabad. Jahangir mentions Aqa Riza, a painter from Herat, to have been in his service while he was a prince. Amongst others, Abu'l Hasan was another famous painter who worked for Jahangir when he was a prince. In his studio the character studies of both people and animals gained popularity.

Under Jahangir and during the larger part of Shah Jahan's reign, Agra remained the capital, though Lahore often shared this honour. It should be mentioned that no illustrated manuscript containing a colophon from Jahangir's atelier at Agra and Lahore is known to have survived. In all likelihood, the miniatures of the *Anwar-i Suhaili* (BM, Add. 18579, datable 1610–11) and the pictures overpainted on the folios in the *Khamsa* of Mir Shir Ali Nawai (RLWC, MS A.8, dateable 1605–11) were executed at Agra. The *Khatirat-i Mutribi Samarqandi*, an account of Mutribi, a Central Asian scholar, shows that the artists were active at Lahore when Jahangir held his court there in 1626.

Before moving his capital to Delhi, Shah Jahan was at Agra from 1628 to 1630. Two manuscripts of this period illustrated at Agra are *Gulistan* (AH 1038/ AD 1628–9, CBL, MS 22) and the *Bostan* of Sa'di (BM, Add. 27262).

Prince Dara Shukoh is known for his great skill in calligraphy and interest in painting. The Dara Shukoh Album (c. 1633–42, IOL, Add. Or. 3129) is a rare collection of the prince's paintings completed during the years 1633–42. Ascriptions on the works of two painters, Anup Chhatr and Chitarman of Shah Jahan's atelier, show that these painters too worked for some time in Dara Shukoh's establishment. A picture of a lady in this album contains the following inscription: *'Amal-i Rai Anup Chhatr Dara Shukohi* (Work of Rai Anup Chhatr [servant] of Dara Shukoh). Rai Anup Chhatr may well have received the title 'Rai' from his patron. Chitarman probably attached himself to Dara Shukoh towards the late 1630s. In one of his signatures on the likeness of Dara Shukoh, he designates himself *Khak-i pa* (Dust under the feet), suggesting that he was in the employment of the prince. The inscription reads: *Khak-i pa Chitarman san 1049*, dated AD 1639–40.

Bernier, who was in Delhi in the early years of Aurangzeb's reign, describes the imperial workshops:

> Large hall are seen in many places, called *Kar-kanays* or workshops for the artisans. In one hall embroiderers are busily employed, superintended by a master. In another you see the goldsmiths; in a third, painters; in a fourth varnishers in lacquer work, in a fifth, joiners, turners, tailors, and shoe-makers; in a sixth, manufacturers of silk, brocade, and those fine muslins of which are made turbans, girdles with golden flowers, and drawers worn by females, so delicately fine as frequently to wear out in one night.

Only a few artists, namely Anup Chhatr, Chhajmal, Ilyas, Bahadur, Ilyas Khan, Lachhman Singh, Muhammad Afzal, and Shamdas, are known to have been active during Aurangzeb's reign.

The Mughal nobles also had their own ateliers. A rare manuscript, *Kitab-i Sa'at* in the Navin Kumar Collection, New York, offers new information. Its colophon reads that it was completed in the library of Khan Azam Mirza Aziz Koka (foster brother of Akbar) at Hajipur in AH 991 (AD 1584). It establishes Mirza's interest in painting and throws light on the atelier attached to his library. The atelier of Abdur Rahim Khan-i Khanan is particularly well known to art historians owing to the description in his biography, *Ma'asir-i Rahimi* ('Abdu-l Baqi Nihawandi 1616), and the survival of the illustrated manuscripts prepared at his library. According to an inscription in the hand-writing of Abdur Rahim Khan-i Khanan on the fly-leaf of the manuscript *Ramayana* (FGA, no. 07.271), it is clear that in or about 1598–9 Mullah Shikebi Imami was holding the charge of manuscript illustration at his library.

According to the *Ain-i Akbari* (Abu'l Fazl 1595), officials called *daroghas* and *bitakchis* supervised the routine work at the atelier. Since the atelier was an integral part of the royal library, both the atelier and the royal library were placed under the command of a darogha. During Jahangir's reign, Makrub Khan was the darogha of the library and the 'Painting House' (*Darogha-i kitabkhana wa naqqashkhana*). He held office from the beginning of Jahangir's reign to virtually its end. Later, during Shah Jahan's reign, Mir Sayyid Ali, the son of Sayyid Jalal, was appointed darogha of the *kitabkhana* and *naqqashkhana* upon the death of Salih Khushnavis. Clearly, the 'Painting House' continued to be attached to the imperial library.

Imperial patronage drew a large number of artists from different regions to the royal studio. Only a few are mentioned in the historical works of the period, but a large number of painters are known from the ascriptions on the miniatures. The place names sometimes accompanying the artists' names give us an indication of their home towns or regions. For instance, painters who came from Kashmir and Gujarat are designated 'Kashmiri' and 'Gujarati' respectively. We find references to Ahmad Kashmiri and Shankar Gujarati. Appendix 1 at the end of this chapter lists such names. Gujarat led the list with nine painters, while Kashmir contributed six, Lahore two, and Gwalior one. Nine painters were from Iran or Central Asia. This, of course, is only a partial list confined to those about whose origins we have definite information.

Some Hindu painters came from low castes and the artisan class. Four (Daswant, Asi, Kesav, and Paras) were *kahar* (palanquin-bearer) and one, Khiman, was a stonemason (*sangtarash*).

The survey of Mughal miniatures yields a total of 327 known painters of whom 260 belong to Akbar's atelier. The break-up by reign is given in Table 1.1.

TABLE 1.1

Reign	Number of artists	
	Hindu	Muslim
Babur (1526–30)	–	–
Humayun (1530–9; 1550–6)	–	6
Akbar (1556–1605)	145	115
Jahangir (1605–27)	43	41
Shah Jahan (1628–58)	17	18
Aurangzeb (1659–1707)	8	4

The total number of painters during Jahangir's reign was only one-third of the painters under Akbar. There was a further decline in their number during Shah Jahan's reign. During Akbar's reign, the Mughal school was at a nascent stage, so artists were drawn to the imperial atelier from various regions, thereby swelling their numbers. By the end of Akbar's reign, specific branches of painting had emerged with distinct characteristics. Jahangir's reign witnessed specialization, notably portrait painting and pictures of flora and fauna, so there was no scope for the lesser-skilled or middle-rung artists. Consequently, several Mughal painters had to seek their fortune outside the imperial atelier, and their work, in general, gave rise to the 'Popular or Sub-imperial Mughal School'. The decreasing number of artists during Shah Jahan's reign may be explained by his overwhelming interest in architecture. It seems plausible that after an almost total shift from manuscript painting to album pictures (especially portraits) during the seventeenth century, the painters lacking excellence in portraiture lost their position at the royal atelier.

A record of each painter's works was maintained at the atelier to determine his progress. Abu'l Fazl says that the work of all painters was laid before Akbar by the daroghas and the clerks on a weekly basis; he then conferred rewards according to the excellence of workmanship, or increased the monthly salaries. Under the system, special care seems to have been taken at the royal atelier to assign miniatures to painters, especially those executed under the 'joint-work system'. In illustrated manuscripts, artists' names were written on the lower margin presumably by the scribes working at the atelier.

An illustration from the *Akhlaq-i Nasiri* (c. 1590–5) could possibly be a scene of the imperial atelier. It represents scribes and artists at work under the supervision of a senior member of the atelier, and in addition, a helper is also shown outside the corridor, smoothening paper. Their identities are, however, not clear. The red sandstone structure, characteristic of sixteenth-century Mughal architecture, appears as an ideal place for the artists and scribes, as its surroundings comprising plants, flowers, and water channels added to the serenity of the setting. In another instance, a dispersed folio shows two painters at work and a noble leaving with his portrait. Such miniatures are also important for the study of an artist's method of working and his art materials. Sometimes the artists moved out of the atelier to portray an event or to sketch the likeness of an individual. A double-page illustration from the *Masnavi* (AD 1662) of Zafar Khan depicts an artist in a court scene recording the likenesses of the nobles. In addition, the artists accompanied the royal camp whenever the emperor left the capital. The notices on Mansur in Jahangir's memoirs, in the context of the pictures of flowers of the Kashmir valley and of a bird called *saj*, show that painters were available to carry out his orders whenever he left the capital on an expedition or for any other reason. This practice obviously gave rise to authentic historical pictures imbued with realism.

Besides the painters, illuminators, gilders, line-drawers, and bookbinders too found employment in the imperial atelier. Information on the painters' salary is scanty. Abu'l Fazl mentioned that 'many *mansabdars*, *ahadis*, and others, hold appointments in this department. The pay of the foot soldiers varies from 1200-600 *dams*'. It seems that under Akbar (as also during the reigns of his successors), no distinction was made between civil and military employees. Painters of a higher status were therefore assigned *mansabs*; others were treated at par with *ahadis* (imperial cavalrymen); and the inferior artists were paid a salary equivalent to that of infantrymen. If the pagers, line-drawers, margin ornamentors, and gilders of the atelier held the status of ordinary soldiers, then the salary of a foot soldier, ranging from 600 dams to 1,200 dams per month (that is,

Rupees 15 to 30), might be taken to be the lowest pay of artists in the atelier. Increase in the painters' salaries depended on the quality of work produced by them. Akbar himself examined the works of individual painters and granted awards and promotions on the basis of their merit. Jahangir's strong interest in painting is well recognized. A seventeenth-century miniature bears testimony to this. It shows Jahangir pointing to the details in a picture brought before him. Here, the figure shown holding the miniature was possibly the chief of the atelier or the painter. The scene, set against the backdrop of a simplified, symmetrical, architectural setting accommodating a very small assembly of men, hints at a private assemblage of people. Jahangir must have had personal moments away from courtly life when he met the artists and examined their work.

No information is available about the ranks and salary enjoyed by the Mughal painters. The high ranks enjoyed by Abdu-s Samad and Muhammad Sharif were exceptions. We know that Khwaja Abdu-s Samad held a mansab of 400 (*zat*) at Akbar's court and in the 22nd regnal year (1578) was the head of the mint at Fatehpur Sikri. Later, in 1585, he was appointed to oversee the sale of leather articles; and in 1587 was appointed

Diwan of Multan. These assignments might possibly have been obtained by Abdu–s Samad because of the favour he enjoyed as an artist, but the principal factor was his family background, as his father was a high Safavid official. For similar reasons, his son Muhammad Sharif, a painter, eventually reached virtually the highest position possible in the Mughal empire. After his accession, Jahangir appointed him *Amir ul Umara* and gave him the rank of 5,000 zat and 5,000 *sawar*. Details are not available for other masters like Mir Sayyid Ali, Basawan, Abu'l Hasan, Aqa Riza, Mansur, Bishandas, and Govardhan in particular, and other painters in general.

An important and influential painter in the Mughal atelier supervised the work. As mentioned, the task of illustrating the *Hamzanama* was initially entrusted to Mir Sayyid Ali and later, when Mir Sayyid Ali left India on a pilgrimage to Mecca, it was assigned to Khwaja Abdu–s Samad. The pictorial colophon of the *Razmnama* (SMS) bears the following inscription: *ba-ihtimam-i murid dar chahar martaba ikhlas pa-bar-ja, Sharif-i Abdu-s Samad surat-i itmam yaft* (Under the supervision of the [Emperor's] disciple, steadfast on all the four stages of sincerity, Sharif, son of Abdu–s

Samad, this attained completion). The date of this manuscript is 1584–5, after the death of Daswant, a principal illustrator of the work. Does this mean then that Muhammad Sharif also held the position of the supervisor of the mint at Fatehpur Sikri, which was placed under the charge of his father in the 22nd regnal year (1578). The *Khamsa* of Nizami (BM, Or. 12208) contains a colophon dated 40th regnal year (1595–6): *ba-ihtimam-i murid dar chahar martaba ikhlas pa-bar-ja, Sharif surat-i itmam paziraft. Wassalam* (Under the supervision of the [Emperor's] disciple who is steadfast in the four stages of sincerity, Sharif, this attained completion. Salutations). Muhammad Sharif continued to hold this responsible position till 1596–7. It was in 1602 that he left the imperial court to join Prince Salim at Allahabad.

An interesting practice that developed at Akbar's atelier was that of joint work. The making of a picture was generally divided into two successive stages, that is, sketching or drawing (*tarh*) and colouring (*'amal* or *rangamezi*). While one painter sketched, another undertook the colouring. Sometimes, a third painter finished the principal figures (*surat*) or portraits (*chihranami*). Line-drawing seems to have held the most important place at the Mughal atelier. This task was usually assigned to skilled master painters. Foremost amongst them were Basawan, Daswant, Kesav, Kanha, Jagan La'l, Mahesh, Miskin, Mukund, Tara, and Tulsi. Most of them have been mentioned by Abu'l Fazl as the leading painters of Akbar's court. The work of colouring was considered secondary to the 'sketch', and therefore was perhaps assigned to less-skilled artists. The practice of collaboration, beyond doubt, gave an opportunity to budding artists to receive instructions in the methods of painting and to learn various disciplines in art from the master painters. Abu'l Fazl tells us that Daswant, whose talent was noticed by Akbar, was placed under the guidance of Khwaja Abdu-s Samad and within a short time he surpassed all painters to become the foremost master painter of his age. Abu'l Fazl adds that Khwaja Abdu-s Samad's other pupils also became masters, though their names are not cited. The practice of correction by a master painter is confirmed by inscriptions on a few miniatures. An illustration in the *Darabnama* (BM, Or. 4615, f.103) carries the inscription: *'Amal-i Bihzad, islah Khwaja Abdu-s Samad* (Work of Bihzad, corrected by Khwaja Abdu-s Samad). Another inscription in the *Baburnama* (BM,

Or. 3714, f.271) reads: *'Amal-i Tirpal, islah Sanwala* (Work of Tirpal, corrected by Sanwala). Thus, master painters examined and improved works executed by younger or less-skilled painters who were presumably their pupils. Sometimes, family connections were also responsible for such collaboration: Nanha, an uncle of Bishandas, executed portraits for his nephew's work.

Such collaborations between senior artists and apprentices was undoubtedly indispensable for forming an independent though composite style of art in the Mughal school. The efforts of artists drawn from diverse regions and brought up in different traditions could be coordinated to achieve an overall homogeneity where various elements were harmoniously reconciled. Under these conditions it was natural that the artists influenced one another and within a short span of time a unified and distinctive style emerged.

It also appears that the system of collaboration in single miniatures, which initially acknowledged the skill of painters in specialized areas of painting, eventually disappeared during the seventeenth century when the Mughal style matured and the divergence of the different traditions of art had been absorbed. Jahangir's claim that he could identify an individual artist's share in a joint work need not be taken as evidence to support the continuity of the system of collaboration in painting during his period:

> As regards myself, my liking for painting and my practice in judging it have arrived at such a point that when any work is brought before me, either of deceased artists or of those of the present day, without the name being told me, I say on the spur of the moment that it is the work of such and such a man. And if there be a picture containing many portraits, and each face be the work of a different master, I can discover which face is the work of each of them. If any other person has put in the eye and eyebrow of a face, I can perceive whose work the original face is, and who has painted the eye and eyebrows.

There is no known instance of such intimate collaboration in the execution of a portrait. The above passage, though commendable in expression, merely demonstrates Jahangir's intimate knowledge of his painters' styles which enabled him to identify a particular painter's work.

The artists are found actively engaged in their profession even at an advanced age. The ascriptions on the miniatures ascribed to Farrukh Beg show that he executed these masterpieces at the age of 70. Mir Musauwir is depicted in his late 70s in his portrait executed by his son Mir Sayyid Ali. Similarly, in the self-portrait executed in 1590 by Kesavdas, he is depicted as a man of advanced age. The long career of the artists at the Mughal atelier can be tentatively ascertained on the basis of their surviving works. The painters, namely Abu'l Hasan, Balchand, Govardhan, and Hashim (or Mir Hashim), had long careers as artists. They were active during the reigns of Akbar, Jahangir, and Shah Jahan.

Appendix 1 List of painters: (i) whose names are given in the ascriptions with the suffix of the names of the places to which they belonged and (ii) whose places of origin are mentioned in the Mughal historical works:

(i)	(ii)
Nand Gawalyari (of Gwalior)	Aqa Riza (of Herat)
Bhim Gujarati (of Gujarat)	Farrukh Beg (of Kabul)
Devjiu Gujarati	Farrukh Qalmaq (Qalmaq, a tribe of Central Asia)
Kesav Gujarati	Khwaja Abdu-s Samad (of Shiraz)
Madhav Gujarati	Maulana Darwesh Muhammad
Prem Gujarati	Maulana Dost
Sarju Gujarati	Maulana Yusuf
Sheoraj Gujarati	Mir Mansur (or Musauwir) (of Tabriz)
Suraj Gujarati	Mir Sayyid Ali (of Tabriz)

Surdas Gujarati
Ahmad Kashmiri (of Kashmir)
Haider Kashmiri
Ibrahim Kashmiri
Kamal Kashmiri
Muhammad Kashmiri
Yaqub Kashmiri
Ibrahim Lahori (of Lahore)
Kalu Lahori
Muhammad Nadir Samarqandi
    (of Samarqand)

2

The Art of Book-illustration

Sixteenth-century Mughal painting may be described essentially as narrative art since it was largely connected with the art of book-illustration. Its roots can be traced to both Persian and Indian art (sculpture as well as painting).

The Mughal school shows the imprint of the Safavid and Timurid art traditions and influences of the classical Indian schools (the Ajanta and western and eastern India schools), especially in the case of manuscript painting: the best and the earliest testimony to this is provided by the illustrations of the *Tutinama* (c. 1565–70, CMA), the *Anwar-i Suhaili* (1570, SOAS), and the *Hamzanama* (c. 1565–80) fragments. A careful study shows that the various modes of visual narration found here continued later in the Mughal school, though with greater complexity. The Mughal pictorial tradition comes out in a variety of ways in the art of book illustration.

It is notable that the literary heritage of a Persian-speaking intelligentsia was never neglected at the Mughal court. Especially under Akbar, copies of Persian classics were made and these were decorated with pictures and border paintings. Abu'l Fazl writes in his *Ain-i Akbari*:

> Persian books, both prose and poetry, were ornament-ed with pictures, and a very large number of paintings was thus collected. The *Story of Hamzah* was repre-sented in twelve volumes, and clever painters made the most astonishing illustrations for no less than one thousand and four hundred passages of the story. The *Chingiznama*, the *Zafarnama*, this book [*Akbarnama*], *Razmnama*, the *Ramayan*, the *Nal Daman*, the *Kalilah Damnah*, the '*Ayar-i Danish*, etc., were all illustrated. (trans. I, 115)

The surviving illustrated manuscripts of Akbar's court exceed the number cited by Abu'l Fazl.

The simplest mode of artistic expression in the Mughal narratives is represented by the illustrations of the *Tutinama*. The key scene from the episode was selected and a brief representation of it was made in one plane. Such scenes are so painted as to enable the viewer to identify the episode. In this manuscript, while a single scene is intended to illustrate one episode, it is of little help to the viewer in understanding the complete story as the earlier and later events do not form any part of the artist's narration. Thus, the representation of a single scene remains isolated and there is no continuity. Consequently, such visual narratives lack the concept of space and time. In these paintings only the key figures of an event appear in a scene and the entire action revolves around them.

The *Tutinama* (CMA) illustrations are thus characterized by 'single-scene' representation, for example, an episode of the 'Thirty-first night' (folio 207r) is represented by how 'the donkey wearing the skin of a tiger, reveals his identify by braying'. The event is thus described:

A merchant had a donkey but no money to buy hay for him. Because of the lack of fodder for the donkey, the merchant was losing business; and the donkey for the lack of oats headed for the storehouse of Judgement Day.

The merchant was a wise man of good deeds. He secured a lion's skin, and every night he put the skin on the donkey and let him wander in the nearby fields and gardens. He instructed him: 'If a watchman appears, bend your left knee and stand still in front of him. Move as much as your coat will allow, but keep him from discovering your real identity. Do not bray so that your disguise is not discovered and thereby your true nature can remain hidden'.

The donkey acted accordingly and fooled everyone. In a few days the donkey recovered and in a short time gained some weight. Since the neighbours thought he was a lion, they abandoned their fields and gardens.

One night the donkey appeared in a certain field. The guards, scared of his claws, climbed up a tree. Just then a donkey nearby brayed. The merchant's donkey, as a donkey would, began to bray also by drawing his breath in and out, making a raucous noise which revealed what he was.

From this harsh sound, the guards discovered what he was and knew what he was not. They descended from the trees, tied the donkey to the tree, gave him a good beating

and punished him for the scare and terror (he had spread).
The animal's own voice had revealed his identity and was the
cause of his disgrace.

The illustrative miniature, while it shows a donkey clad in a tiger's skin (lion's skin in the text) braying amidst a field, and the guards hiding in the foliage of trees, alarmed at the raucous sound made by the animal, illustrates only the part of the story italicized in the above passage.

The naiveté displayed by 'single-scene' representations could be the result of their derivation from the Indian tradition. This characteristic of the *Tutinama* narrative gradually tended to disappear from the works of the Mughal school as the art of visual narration led from the simple to the complex. In 'single-scene' representations, the narrative movements of the text are virtually ignored and, thus, there are always limited possibilities for pictorial action. In such examples, the dramatic aspect of the illustration is the only force that stimulates the viewer to relate it to the story. In some cases (like the illustrations on folios 37v, 43r, 51v, 102v, 223v, 282v, and 316r in this manuscript), the illustrations neither unfold a story nor even depict a part of it.

Their purpose appears didactic and purely decorative. In such cases visual recounting of a scene does not appear to have been the intention of the artist.

The compositions representing continuous narration of an event are sometimes seen in *Anwar-i Suhaili* (SOAS), a manuscript contemporary with the *Tutinama*. Otherwise, in general, this manuscript also contains 'one-scene' representations. In it, within a single picture plane, more than one phase of an event or story is represented. The phases selected for representation are, of course, generally the end or the climax of the story. The artist, however, does not demarcate the two phases and depicts them within a single visual field. The only indication of the identification of these phases is the repetition of the principal figure in various spaces in the composition plotted by the artist. These phases of an event relate the successive movements of the story, and are suggestive of both space and time in the painting. The miniature on folio 232r in *Anwar-i Suhaili* illustrates the story of an old farmer's unfaithful young wife who eloped with a prince. On their way, while they rested near a spring, a lion suddenly attacked the woman and the prince galloped away in terror. In the illustration, the figures of the main characters, the prince and woman, are shown twice. In the composition, in the right-hand corner (below), the prince and the woman are shown seated by a spring; and the left-hand corner depicts the woman being mauled by the lion and the prince galloping away. Thus, these two successive stages of an event are represented in a single visual field to suggest the continuity of the event taking place at different times. The repetition of figures of the main characters in Mughal narrative painting is, however, quite rare; it is also unknown in Persian book-illustration. In Indian art, the earliest evidence of this is found in the Gandhara and Mathura sculptures and examples of this narrative method is seen at the stupas of Sanchi (second half of the first century BC) and in Ajanta paintings. Besides, its continuity is evidenced in the Rajasthani and Pahari schools of painting till the eighteenth century.

Another mode of continuous narration seen in the *Hamzanama* illustrations shows multiple phases of an event depicted within a single visual field. These phases (units of an event) revolve around the central theme and make the representation of the event more elaborate and descriptive. In such instances, the principal figures are not repeated. Rather, the picture plane is divided into small units which contain action related to the main theme. In the division of the visual field, the receptacles comprising hillocks, mounds of earth, a stream, vegetation, architectural columns, and the like, are freely used. This is a technique well known to the Ajanta paintings and Persian manuscript painting.

The general trend in the fifteenth-to-sixteenth-century Persian narrative art was to break up a visual field into two or more units, but these units remained isolated in the absence of any effort on the part of the artist to show any form of association between them. As a result, continuity in the narration suffered. Mughal artists rectified this shortcoming and succeeded in connecting the units through rhythmic movements, gestures, and facial expressions. This introduced freedom, boldness, and vigour in their work which the Persian painters had never been able to achieve. The rhythmic movement not only established a link between the figures but also promoted naturalism. This tie-up between the figures is psychological, in contrast to the almost formal relationship evidenced in Persian painting. The vitality, inner coherence, and unity in the *Hamzanama* illustrations are obviously the result of indigenous elements at work in the formation of the Mughal style. In the narratives of the *Tutinama* too there is an emphasis on establishing a psychological correlation between the figures.

The units within a single frame corresponded to the sequence or a formal order of an event or a story. For example, in a birth scene the units (from top to bottom), interwoven quite naturally to narrate an event, show: (*a*) a queen with her newborn baby attended by her maids; (*b*) musicians and dancers, largely female artistes; (*c*) nobles meeting the emperor to congratulate him on the auspicious occasion; (*d*) astrologers preparing the birth chart, and (*e*) lastly, the performance of the *naqqarkhana* and distribution of alms among the poor. The order is consistently followed, deleting one or two details in the synoptic narration of the event of the birth of a prince. In this mode of narration there is no formal hint at the sequence of the event and the viewer is expected to understand this through the textual references.

The modes of synoptic narration emerged in their most mature form in the illustrations of the *Ta'rikh-i Khandan-i Timuria*, c. 1584–7 (OPL), the *Jami'ut Tawarikh*, dated 1597–8 (IL), and the *Akbarnama*, c. 1602–5 (VA), where we find the visual field in a single illustration accommodating three to five units illustrating the successive progressions of an event. An outstanding example of such an arrangement is an illustration, 'Daughters of Sultan Muhammad being married' in the *Ta'rikh-i Khandan-i Timuria* (f. 40). In this painting the visual field accommodates four units. The upper half, divided diagonally, represents the emperor and the nobles (the latter wishing him on the occasion), and the princesses being attended by their maids. The lower half accommodates musical parties in two separate groups. First, there is a group of female musicians and dancers; and thereafter, outside the palace, the musicians of the naqqarkhana are shown giving performances, while the attendants stand with gifts, and so on, in their hands. Here the units are separated by architectural features (mainly walls) and are set in a series of ascending diagonals in a zigzag order.

In another instance, 'Rejoicings at the birth of Akbar's second son, Murad' in the *Akbarnama* (VA, IS, 2–1896, no. 80/117), the visual field comprises five units: the unit on the top right shows the queen with her newborn baby attended by maids; the unit adjoining it on the extreme top right shows female attendants engaged in some work; the units just below those two units depict female musicians and dancers, while a group of astrologers are busy preparing the horoscope; lastly, the unit at the bottom depicts the musicians of the naqqarkhana performing alongside male dancers outside the palace (see Figure 4).

In some cases, emphasis given to a certain event was explained by treating its various phases as the subjects of separate visual fields. For example, to depict the story of 'The fowler, the pigeons, the mouse, and the crow', the entire sequence of the event is represented in phases and each is the subject of one illustration. These are: (*a*) 'Crow sees a fowler setting his net'; (*b*) 'Flock of pigeons settles on the net'; (*c*) 'Pigeons fly off, carrying the net'; (*d*) 'Mouse releases the pigeons from the net'; and (*e*) 'Crow having seen how helpful the mouse has been to the pigeons, feels a desire to be friends with him'. These miniatures, while they related to a single story and depict its various stages, are treated as independent pictures.

The figures, although shown in a very causal style, extend beyond the picture frame, a marked characteristic of the Safavid and Timurid miniatures, and appear complementary to the mode of continuous narration. Similarly, the objects shown only in part on

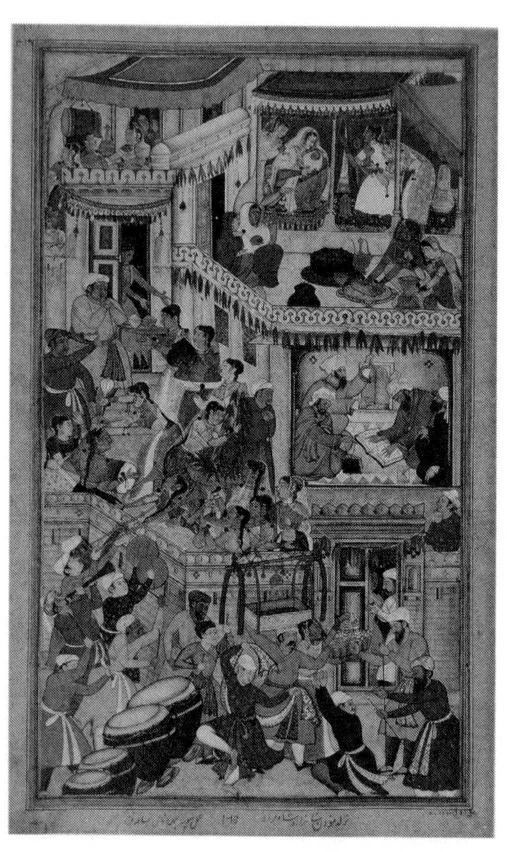

FIGURE 4 Rejoicing at the birth of Akbar's second son, Murad, in 1570. Bhura, portraits by Basawan. Illustration to the *Akbarnama*, c. 1590–5. Victoria and Albert Museum, London (IS 2-1896 80/117).

the extreme outer margin of the visual field, some portion being cut out of vision, are also suggestive of the continuity of the scene beyond the picture frame. The artists have used the picture frame to cut the scene, implying that the viewer is seeing only a part of the whole. This mode undoubtedly imparted breadth to the visual field.

By and large, the Mughal painters composed the various phases of an event in a vertical format, that is, in ascending order. Subsequently, the units of an episode are represented one above the other, separated by receptacles placed in the visual field. In this order, objects are shown simultaneously at eye level (direct-view) and from above (bird's-eye view) in a hierarchical perspective. Stella Kramrisch has called this complexity of views 'multiple perspective'. It marks a definite shift away from the strict Persian convention, the earliest examples of which appear in the *Hamzanama* miniatures with a characteristic treatment of the picture-space—of plane behind plane, that is, subsidiary scenes set in the background, which is a style that is fundamentally Indian, not Persian.

The Mughal painters demonstrated great ingenuity in their narrative while making the fullest use of receptacles to create rhythm. A zigzag placement of small units, rather than their arrangement in a vertical order in a single visual field, suggested movement, and also enhanced the depth of the picture. Similarly, the diagonal setting of objects (main characters) particularly suited action-filled narratives. The visual narratives, largely characterized by the violent physical action and excitement of the *Akbarnama* (VA), demonstrate that artists considered diagonal emphasis more vital than vertical or horizontal ones. The diagonal pull of the thundering elephants seems about to topple the composition in 'Akbar riding the elephant Hawai pursuing another elephant' (VA, IS-2-1896, 22/117), as it threatens to upset the flimsy pontoon bridge (see Figure 5). The fleeing Ran Bagh even crosses the picture frame, which adds further tension to the whole composition. We find this bold diagonal axis repeated in other illustrations from the *Akbarnama*. It appears to have been a favourite compositional device. This painting is certainly one of the most powerfully conceived and executed in the entire *Akbarnama* manuscript.

In spite of the limitations of the narrative styles, there was always a great variety in the artist's mode of expression even in the depiction of narratives on

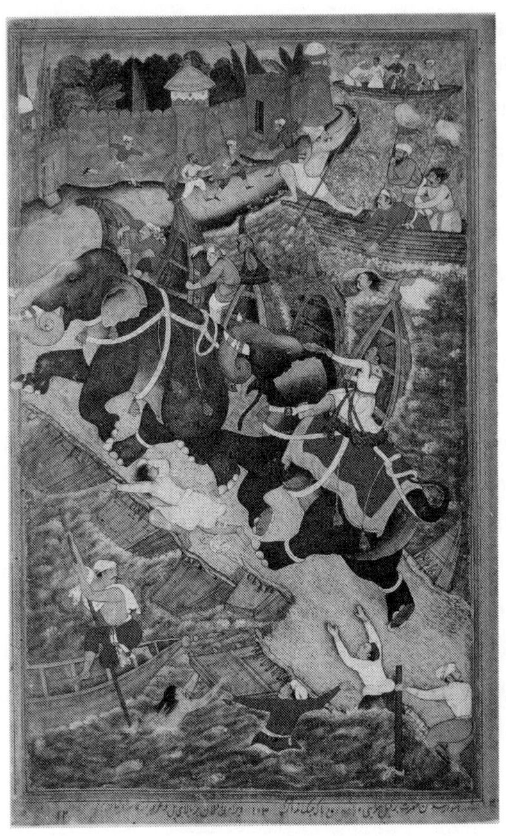

FIGURE 5 Akbar riding the elephant Hawai pursuing another elephant, by Basawan and Chetar. Illustration to the *Akbarnama*, c. 1590–5. Victoria and Albert Museum, London (IS 2-1896 22/117).

similar themes, and he seems to have enjoyed considerable freedom in the selection of descriptive details related to the main event. A comparison of four miniatures from the various copies of the *Baburnama* in the British Museum, London; National Museum, New Delhi; Museum of Oriental Art, Moscow; and Fogg Art Museum, Cambridge—all representing a single event (bird-trapping)—would confirm that the pictures differed in the details of the objects. In them, the scene is located amidst a rocky landscape with a net spread out in the middle of the composition. The bird-trappers, who sit hiding behind a tree, or a mound of earth, or a thatched screen, hold the strings of the net. Strikingly, the 'decoy-bird', which beguiled other birds to descend on the net fixed on the ground, is shown perched on a stand placed in the middle of the net. All the four illustrations show a variety of birds descending, unaware of the fowler and the trap laid for them. The visual relates to the text: 'Bird catching is their trade: they dig tanks, set decoy-birds on them, put a net over the middle, and in this way take all sorts of birds'.

One finds that the British Museum miniature is more elaborate as it represents bird-trappers in action with a variety of devices used in trapping. It also shows a group of men witnessing the scene, one of whom carries a falcon to hunt birds. Babur noted that trained falcons were employed to hunt cranes and other birds. The articles used by bird-trappers, for example, the glued stick, cages, and baskets to hold the trapped birds, are also depicted. As against this, the illustrations at the National Museum (New Delhi) and Moscow collections are comparatively simple in detail as well as composition. However, a stream in the foreground is a common feature. Thus, the number of objects introduced in a visual field and other details comprising the background always varied even in narratives with identical themes.

A miniature on this theme from the *Baburnama* manuscript at the Fogg Art Museum invites additional attention. It displays bird-trappers in three groups hiding behind thatched screens. The 'decoy-bird' can be seen in the middle of the net spread in the central part of the composition. The bird-trapper depicted in the foreground pulls the strings of the net, trapping the birds. The representation of another bird-trapper using a long stick with glued upper end to catch the birds is an additional detail provided by the artist. Besides, the sparsely grown trees with dense foliage and the variety of birds perched on them and hovering over the nets complement the theme, imparting a lively spirit to the picture. One, thus, finds that artists narrated the theme in the light of their personal contemporary experience and observation.

Besides, in the selection of the event, too, the artist had a choice. This becomes clear after a comparison of miniatures illustrating a single event and an appreciation of their content in the light of the literal demands of the text. One such example is 'Akbar on his way to Pak Patan hunting wild asses', illustrated in the *Ta'rikh-i Khandan-i Timuria* (c. 1584–7) and *Akbarnama* (c. 1602–5). This particular event is thus described by Abu'l Fazl (1601) in his *Akbarnama* (trans. II, 522):

> On the way a strange thing occurred on the borders of Rai 'Ala'ud-din's Talondi near the Sutlaj, which is there called the Harhari. The brief account of this is that the scouts reported that there was a herd of wild asses (*gorkhar*). The sovereign proceeded to hunt them, attended by three or four special huntsmen. When he came near the plain he dismounted and proceeded on foot. At the first shot he hit an ass, and the rest of the herd fled far away at the report of the gun. That Divine world-hero took his piece in his hand and proceeded

rapidly on foot over the burning sand, attended by the same three or four huntsmen. He soon traversed the plain and camp up with the herd and killed one after the other with his gun. He continued to follow them up, and on that day he shot thirteen wild asses. Whenever he killed one the others went further off than at first. At this time he became consumed by thirst. There was no sign of water. As he had decided to follow the prey on foot, those attached to the hunt thought that H.M. was near at hand, and so kept in view the place where the game was and did not leave their place. When the lord of the world had traversed some *kos*, his attendants, though they searched, could get no news of the water-carriers, nor any trace of water. A strange condition supervened, and the weakness from thirst increased to such a degree that he lost the power of speech.

The miniature in the former manuscript, depicting Akbar on foot engaged in hunting wild asses with his matchlock, is a visual narration of the first part of the event. The second and concluding phase of the event is the choice of the *Akbarnama* artists, Mahesh and Kesav. They represent Akbar seated and exhausted after the hunt, his matchlock resting on his shoulder, and the attendants enquiring about the emperor's condition. Thus, while the event remains the same, the choice is varied in the selection of the part of an episode to be illustrated. The selection, of course, is always related to a crucial part of the episode which enables the viewer to relate to the story.

Often, to lay emphasis on a particular event, the visual field is enlarged by making the composition a double-page illustration. The theme 'Battle between the rival groups of sanyasis at Thanesar' forms a one-page illustration in the *Ta'rikh-i Khandan-i Timuria* (c. 1584–7) and represents the principal characters at the centre of the visual field, and the battle-scene on the right-hand corner. A double-page illustration of the same event, executed during 1602–5 in the *Akbarnama*, is clearly much richer in descriptive detail. The location of the battle in both the visual narratives is identical, that is, the huge banyan tree at the centre of the masonry platform by the side of a large tank, beside which all the action is shown to be taking place. The *Akbarnama* illustration contains more detail in conformity with the text of the event described by Abu'l Fazl. It shows Akbar's men joining one group (Puris) of sanyasis in their attack on the rival group (Kurs), and

Anand Kur, the chief of the latter group, being slain. Thus, one finds that the above two historical illustrations, though executed in a different space and time, adhered to the text in its essence. This characteristic of visual narrations also confirms their historical nature.

The Mughal visual narratives are at variance with their counterparts in pre-Mughal Indian art. There is a clear departure from the traditional didactic function of the illustrations, as seen in the illustrated manuscripts of the western India school (and also in the early Mughal *Tutinama* manuscript), where incorporation of the illustrations seems merely decorative and simply serves as a vehicle to enhance the appeal of the text. At the Mughal atelier, representation of actual narrative details became the mainstay of an artist's work. He always seemed particular about the accuracy and truthful depiction of the objects relating to the descriptive details of a scene or event. His visual narratives are well recognized for a faithful depiction of material culture and natural history. While looking at them today, one finds oneself transported into the past. Of course, in the case of past events the artist had no opportunity of directly experiencing visual contact with the events, unlike the portrayal of contemporary episodes and events. In such narratives, the descriptive details in the visual field are expanded by the artist by drawing upon his experience as well as imagination which was further enlivened by naturalism. By placing the main characters of an event in their appropriate surroundings, the Mughal artist created drama in the visual field to meet the literal illustrative demand of the text.

It seems that Jahangir had little interest in manuscript painting. It also has to be mentioned that the most important manuscript, the *Akbarnama*, copies of which were taken up for illustration during the late 1590s, was never fully illustrated. The manuscripts of the *Akbarnama* (datable 1604) in the Chester Beatty Library, Dublin; the British Museum and Library, London; and the Victoria & Albert Museum, London, close with an account of the years 1556–80/1, 1542–55, and 1562–77/8, respectively. Though the imperial status of the British Museum copy is clear, as it bears Jahangir's note that its scribe was Muhammad Husain of Kashmir 'Zarrin Qalam', and also because its first two folios were illuminated with broad margin-painting at Jahangir's studio. However, Jahangir never planned to have the remaining part of the *Akbarnama* text, that is, 1581–1605, illustrated. Also, neither the illustrations of a fragmentary copy of the *Akbarnama* (early Jahangir school) in the Gulistan Palace Library, Tehran, nor the astray folios of the *Akbarnama* in the India Office Library, London, and Edwin Binney 3rd Collection, Portland, illustrate the events of the latter part of Akbar's reign. It may be mentioned that no illustrated copy of the *Tuzuk-i Jahangiri* is known, though Jahangir's statement, 'As these animals appeared to me very strange, I both described them and ordered that painters should draw them in the *Jahangirnama*', assures us that illustrated copies of the emperor's memoirs were prepared. We know that the work of illustrating the *Jahangirnama* was in progress in 1618 from Jahangir's specific mention of the illustrated frontispiece, namely the scene of Jahangir's accession painted by Abu'l Hasan that year. Barely two months after that event, the first copy of the *Jahangirnama* was presented to Shah Jahan, and a little later that very year, two copies were presented to Itimaduddaula and Asaf Khan. There is, however, no specific evidence that the gifted copies contained illustrations, and no illustrated manuscript is known that is datable after 1610–15 from Jahangir's studio. Thus, it seems that the principal emphasis was on album pictures.

The seventeenth century witnessed a marked shift in line with the royal patrons' interest in album pictures, that is, portraits, natural history paintings, genre scenes, and the like. The illustrations of the two manuscripts, the *Bostan* of Sa'di (BM, Add. 27262) and the *Gulistan* of Sa'di (CBL, Indian MS. 22), datable 1628–30 and executed at Shah Jahan's atelier at Agra, clearly show diminishing artistic accomplishment. In them, the illustrations, composed in an almost square or horizontal format with large calligraphy, appear unappealing. In addition, the miniatures are too small for the size of the manuscripts concerned.

Here the illustrations of the *Padshahnama*, c. 1657 (RLWC) deserve especial mention. There appears to be an assemblage of pictures suitable for its embellishment. Some were executed at Jahangir's studio (which also form a part of this manuscript). This points to a continuance of manuscript painting with a diminished and lukewarm interest. There are also illustrations from the late eighteenth and early nineteenth centuries, most likely executed at the Oudh centres of painting (Lucknow and Faizabad). These appear to have been incorporated in the copy when it was rebound. It is

not clear whether such illustrations replaced the origi-
nals or were new additions.

This copy of the *Padshahnama* is also incomplete
and those illustrations that relate to the Mughal school
do not cover the full account of the *Padshahnama*
compiled by Abdul Hamid Lahori. There is no doubt
that the enormous number of book-illustrations, and
so thematically varied, produced at Akbar's studio is
unprecedented in the history of Indian art.

3

Portraiture

Portrait painting, widely practised in classical Indian art, flourished at the Mughal atelier by blending characteristics of Persian and European art with traditional Indian art, along with an element of originality. The Mughal artists' special emphasis on the delineation of the characteristic details was the basis of the formation and development of a definite style of portraiture. Babur's comment on the portraits executed by Bihzad, 'Of the painters, one was Bihzad. His work was very dainty but he did not draw beardless faces well; he used greatly to lengthen the double chin (*ghab-ghab*); bearded faces he drew admirably', is illustrative of the Mughal patron's desire for an exact rendering of the facial contours, or the likeness of an individual.

His grandson Jahangir, too, provided precise descriptions of an individual's appearance. About his father, the emperor Akbar, he writes:

> In his august personal appearance he was of middle height, but inclining to be tall; he was of hue of wheat; his eyes and eyebrows were black, and his complexion rather dark than fair. He was lion-bodied, with a broad chest, and his hands and arms long. On the left side of his nose he had a fleshy mole, very agreeable in appearance; of the size of half a pea.

These 'pen-pictures' suggest a definite preference of the Mughal patrons for lifelike representations. In this context, the definition of a picture (*taswir*), by Abu'l Fazl, is relevant: 'Drawing the likeness of anything is called *taswir*.' It was Akbar himself, who in line with his genius for innovation and love of history (as witnessed in Abu'l Fazl's great historical work, the *Akbarnama*), ordered an album of portraits of his nobles to be prepared. The emperor was so anxious to have authentic portraits that he especially sat for the painter who drew his likeness.

A pictorial colophon in the *Khamsa* of Nizami (BM, Or. 12208, dated 1596–7, folio 325b) shows an artist,

Daulat, executing the likeness of the scribe Abdur Rahim, seated before him. In another instance, the *Masnavi* of Zafar Khan (RAS, dated 1662) contains a double-page illustration which shows an artist drawing the likeness of the nobles present at Zafar Khan's court. This pictorial evidence confirms that the Mughal artists drew the portraits of individuals from life.

The album of portraits from Akbar's studio does not seem to have survived. Nevertheless, a fair number of Mughal portraits from his time are available that fairly represent the achievements of the sixteenth-century artists. Jahangir, like his father, also had portraits made of his nobles, which he gathered together in albums.

The single-figure portrait, greatly in vogue during the seventeenth century, had its genesis at Akbar's atelier. A few single portraits known from his atelier show in general the figure in profile, standing in isolation against a flat ground painted pale green (see Figure 6). In this context, amongst the earliest groups, is the portrait of Prince Daniyal (c. 1595, MMA, no. 55.121.10.32r), executed by Manohar. A later inscription (Jahangir's autograph) given on it authenticates the identity of the prince. The inscription reads: *Shabih-i biradaram Daniyal marhum manand ast* (An exact likeness of my late brother Daniyal). In the portrait, rendering of the contours of the body appear somewhat stiff rather than natural. However, these contours reveal the physiognomy of an athlete. Another study of this prince is available in the Chhatrapati Shivaji Maharaj Vastu Sangrahalaya, Mumbai. Both these portraits are in rigid profile, which hints at the beginning of a shift from a three-quarter view to profile in portraiture by the end of the sixteenth century. Later, full profile became a characteristic trait of Mughal portraits. In both the above pictures, however, the facial features and physical appearance are virtually identical; the difference lies in the positioning of the hands, and also in the shape of the *jama* (a double-breasted coat). In the latter example, the jama's skirt is shown as being round rather than having slits at the hem.

Next is the portrait of Raja Suraj Singh Rathore (c. 1596–1600, MMA, no. 55.121.10.7r), executed by Bishandas. His portrait, drawn in profile, is also shown silhouetted against a pale green background, which clearly seems to have been expanded when the picture was remargined at a later date. An inscription, in all likelihood written by Shah Jahan, on the lower margin of the illustrated mount reads: *Shabih-i Raja Suraj Singh*

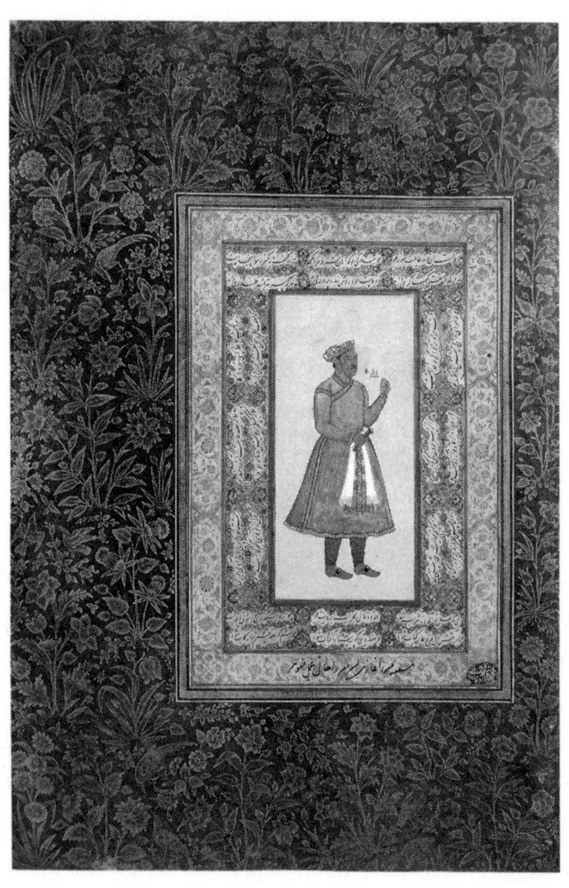

FIGURE 6 Mirza Ghazi (d. 1612). By Manohar, c. 1610–12. Bequeathed by Lady Wantage. Victoria and Albert Museum, London (IM, 118-1921).

Rathore, kar-i Bishandas (Likeness of Raja Suraj Singh Rathore, work of Bishandas). Another portrait of this raja, known in Jahangir Album (SLB), again in profile, and also executed by Bishandas, bearing Jahangir's autograph dated AH 1017/AD 1608, is datable to the 1590s. Jahangir describes it as a 'very close likeness (*shabih*)'. Both portraits bear close affinity in style and show a striking resemblance in terms of the features of the raja. In them, the Mughal artist's talent in presenting the delicate technical fineness in portraiture is evident. Needless to say, Bishandas, who earned a singular reputation in portrait painting during Jahangir's reign, had already established himself in this branch of painting by the end of the sixteenth century. This can be inferred from the comparison of Bishandas' work with the portrait of Raja Suraj Mal (IM) executed by his uncle Nanha, a senior painter at Akbar's studio. Bishandas clearly excelled Nanha in these portraits. Nevertheless, both painters aimed at realistic representation of the subject. It is also evident from the portraits that the aim was to reveal the character and personality of the subject.

Other known famous single-figure-type portraits are those of Tansen, Raisal Darbari, Raja Man Singh,

Mota Raja Udai Singh of Jodhpur, Rai Singh of Bikaner, and Safdar Khan. A portrait of Tansen (c. 1590–1600) is preserved in the Chrysler Museum of Art, Norfolk, Virginia (58.27.20). Here the figure, set against a flat green background, is characteristic of the Mughal style of the sixteenth century. The positioning and posture of the figures appear formalized, drawn on set lines, with the face in full profile and the remaining part of the body in three-quarter view, while both the hands with palms clasped rest on a long staff in consonance with the slightly leaning posture. Similar positioning of figures can be seen in other contemporary portraits of Raisal Darbari (c. 1590–5) and Raja Man Singh (c. 1600–5). The likeness of the musician is identified from the inscription given across the bottom of the long white jama. It reads: *Shabih-i Tansen* (Likeness of Tansen). The practice of including the inscriptions on some part of the figure itself to disclose the identity of the subject was rarely adopted at Akbar's studio. Later, during the seventeenth century, it became a common practice and minute inscriptions disclosing the identity of individuals, especially in group portraits, appear quite frequently. In another painting, an almost identical portrait of Tansen (NM), he appears in a long white jama reaching below the ankles and fastened round the waist with a long girdle (*katzeb* or *patka*) and with a dagger tucked into it. Here, the hands shown in action to give voice to the music lend the picture a lyrical quality, which in turn tends to be a psychological portrait. Here too, the figure is shown isolated against a simple green background. These portraits indicate that Tansen was a tall and slim man with a darkish complexion.

In the portrait of Raisal Darbari (c. 1590–5, CBL, MS. 44, no. 2) the figure is drawn in a pose virtually identical to Tansen's portrait, with the difference that it is composed in the reverse order so that the figure looks to the left. The miniature bears an inscription on the top: *Surat-i Raisal Darbari* (Likeness of Raisal Darbari). As usual, the figure is depicted against a solitary background and the face is portrayed in strict profile. A long sheet of cloth (*chadar*) thrown around the shoulders with its ends hanging loosely is an essential part of a noble's dress. Its treatment, with heavy rhythmic folds and with deep shading, testify to the influence of European art.

The portrait of Raja Man Singh (c. 1600–5, MMA) is also of the formal type in line with the portraits of Tansen and Raisal Darbari. This favourite 'type' of portraiture continued to be made in the seventeenth century. It was a unique style of the Mughal artist: a full figure with head turned to one side in full profile, or three-quarter, or, rarely, one-quarter. The full figure revealed an individual's personality and his sartorial habits. Besides physical appearance, these portraits also provide invaluable visual documentation of social and cultural history of the period. Since the contemporary chronicles are generally silent on these points, the portraits fill this lacuna to some extent.

By and large, the portraits of Akbar's atelier show the central figure set against a flat background and the face represented in profile. Mention may be made of a portrait of Rai Singh of Bikaner (c. 1590–1600, Private Collection), where the figure is set against a flat green background but the face is in one-and-a-quarter view, which is uncommon in Mughal portraiture. This is a trend possibly linked to the last phase of the disappearance of the further-eye of the western India school, where, in full profile, the second eye is projected beyond the facial contours. Also, in the manuscript paintings of Akbar's court, facial expression in one-and-a-quarter view was common and the second eye was drawn protruding slightly beyond the outline of the face.

The portraits of persons other than royalty are a class in themselves and offer even more insight into the development of portraiture. In this context, Basawan, whom Abu'l Fazl considered a master painter excelling in various branches of painting, including the 'drawing of features' (portraits), is in the forefront. His masterpieces include 'Flute-player' (c. 1590), 'Dervish' (c. 1590), and 'Jain ascetic' (c. 1590–5). In the lyrical portrait, the flute-player, shown against a flat ground, is dramatically posed as if dancing to the tune being played by him on the flute (MG). The heavily folded, long flowing sheet of cloth thrown across the shoulders also creates a rhythmic pattern. This portrait is undoubtedly superb in its rendering of the mood of the musician, delineating his physical features, and in its stress on modelling and presentation of mass and volume.

Another presentation of a real character is Basawan's portrait of a wandering dervish (MG). In this portrait the lively facial features with intense gaze, and the slightly bent, lean, and emaciated figure imbued with gentle movement are unexpectedly natural. This realism, of course, distinguishes Mughal painting from the mannered style of portraiture of the Persian school. The portrait of a Jain ascetic (CMA, Basawan's name given on it is partly erased), too, is unusual since it is imbued with psychological insight. The holy man, clad in a white flowing costume (dhoti) and a long transparent sheet of white cloth covering his shoulders, is depicted on his way somewhere, carrying holy books under his arm (CMA). His facial features indicate that he is in deep meditation and engrossed in personal thoughts. The gentle movement of the cloth suggests a morning breeze flowing across the figure. These remarkable studies show Basawan's genius in the grasp of the qualities of a genuine portrait. His art set a high benchmark in expressive portrait painting that only a few Mughal painters could attain.

Mansur is another artist who expanded the ambit of portrait painting with a touch of originality. The portrait of a *vina*-player (c. 1600) preserved in the collection of Edward Croft Murray, London, is a psychological study in which he has successfully captured the musician's feelings, a rare quality in portraiture that only a few other painters from Akbar's studio, namely Basawan, La'l, Manohar, and Daulat, were able to achieve. In this painting the musician's reclining head over the vina (a plucked string instrument) relates the interaction between the ears and the sound emanating from the resonators of the instrument held diagonally. This adds a lyrical quality to the portrait. The study also hints at a further evolution in the treatment of the background. Rising flowering plants forming an arcade over the human figure hint at vertical movement, a rare phenomenon in the portraits of Akbar's reign. Though no definite horizon line is shown, the depiction of rows of birds at a high margin suggests an aerial perspective.

Another portrait of a huntsman holding a falcon (c. 1600–5, LACM), probably a work by Mansur, also shows a flight of birds on the high margin denoting an aerial perspective. In the latter example the background is flat but with an introduction of a vanishing high horizon line at the top. These two examples suggest the introduction of landscape elements in the handling of space in portrait painting. This practice finds its full fruition during the seventeenth century in the works of Bichitr, Govardhan, and Payag.

Basawan's and Mansur's works clearly establish a genre in Mughal portraiture and epitomizes the art of portraiture in Mughal painting. The Mughal painters reveal a deep understanding of the character and the psychology of ordinary people, which was aptly reflected in the portraits. La'l is another prolific painter of Akbar's court who successfully captured human moods and feelings in his portraits. His painting 'An old man writing in a book, seated in a landscape' (c. 1590–1600) clearly reflects strain in the old man's face.

Historical double/group portraits, too, originated during the sixteenth century. The best known picture in this category was probably 'Akbar's illness in old age' (c. 1605, CAM), executed by Manohar Das. In this painting the artist has concentrated on the psychological relationship between the participants in the scene. Akbar, as an old man, appears in the three-quarter view. This sensitive actual portrait, painted towards the end of Akbar's life, served as a model for his posthumous pictures executed during the seventeenth and eighteenth centuries. The painter's success is evident from the expressions depicted on the faces, strikingly revealing their moods and feelings in response to the event. The hand gestures and physical action, redolent of the slow movement in the picture, imparts a lively and natural ambience to the scene. Such penetrating psychological portrayal of people was one of the great achievements of the Mughal school. A sense of sadness pervades the entire picture, as a grim-faced Akbar gazes into the eyes of the person (possibly Hakim Ali Gilani) attending on him, who comforts him with some comment. The gravity of the situation is well reflected in the portraits of the princes Khurram and Khusrau standing behind the emperor. Their facial expressions and hand gestures reveal their anxiety. This somber situation is, however, relieved by the entry of a huntsman.

Another outstanding example of the double portrait is Basawan's 'A mulla argues with a dervish' (AD 1595, BLO), in which the artist realistically depicts the confrontation between the two men. In this double portrait, Basawan has succeeded in presenting human feelings with theatrical effect. The dervish, though engaging in the conversation, is represented as being calm, at ease, and engrossed in his work. It lends the figure a mysterious quality and is undoubtedly a wonderfully naturalistic depiction of the subject. The depiction of the mulla arguing a point, with his left arm stretched and pointing towards the dervish, communicates a linkage between the two. It is to the artist's credit that the features are true to life and the dramatic effect of the interaction between the two is emphatically achieved.

This group portrait is a remarkable example of the development of this genre. The simplicity of the composition suggests that the Mughal artist concentrated primarily on the subject and graphically captured lively moments recreated from life.

Portraiture at the imperial Mughal atelier developed with a marked tenor of realism (altogether absent in Persian painting) in the depiction of physical features, moods, feelings, and rhythm. However, the most important feature was the emphasis on accuracy in terms of the minutest details in delineating the contours of body and the true-to-life representation of the subject. These trends continued in the later period, undoubtedly with greater clarity and in their established form. The shift from the three-quarter view to the full profile in portraiture, already observed during Akbar's reign, was complete in Jahangir's and Shah Jahan's ateliers where portraits in rigid profile dominate. The treatment of the background with elements of landscape become more frequent. Nevertheless, the fashion of depicting figures against a flat, solitary ground remained in vogue throughout the period of the Mughal school. Similarly, the most popular genre, the single-figure-type portrait and the double or group portrait, with its roots in Akbar's atelier, reached its height during the seventeenth century. The most significant genre of the Mughal school, the portrayal of the life of common people, owes its development to Akbar's studio. The works of Basawan remained unsurpassed even during later times. Only a few painters of the seventeenth-century Mughal atelier, namely Daulat, Govardhan, Bichitr, Abu'l Hasan, and Payag, were his match. In Mughal portraits, the emphasis was on the individualization of facial features and expression so that every human figure became more or less identifiable.

It is also noteworthy that the portraits of ordinary people are spontaneous pictures, altogether different from the stately ones of the royalty or nobles, which are largely mannered, typified, and stereotyped both in positioning and posture. This formalized expression, however, does not adversely affect the sensitive portrayal of the characteristic features of the subject. The spontaneous portraits are studies focused largely on the presentation of a particular mood and action and are extraordinarily intimate psychological portraits. Here, the artist seems to have a close understanding of the subject and his character. This relationship of the artist with the subject allowed him to deviate from the prescribed conventions in drawing and composition and resulted in the spontaneity in the artist's expression. Hence, portraits of ordinary men are full of life and warmth, resulting in works that are true to nature. Creativity and originality in portraiture could well be assessed on the basis of this particular group of portraits. In this context, Havell's remark on a miniature, '*Rubab* player, his companion, and a peasant' (c. 1615–20, VA, IM, 27 & A-1925) ascribed to Bichitr (see Figure 7), is relevant:

> A one-eyed musician is singing with great gusto a song which excites the hilarity of his listener, the bowman holding an arrow in his left hand and apparently beating time with his right foot. The facial expression of both is admirably rendered, and the imperturbable countenance of the servant (obviously a villager) squatting in the foreground with his bundle, between the legs, is equally true of his life.

Emblematic and Allegorical Portraits

Till Akbar's reign, no symbols were attached to the portrait of an individual, or other subjects, with the exception of an aureole, the symbol of divine light, and

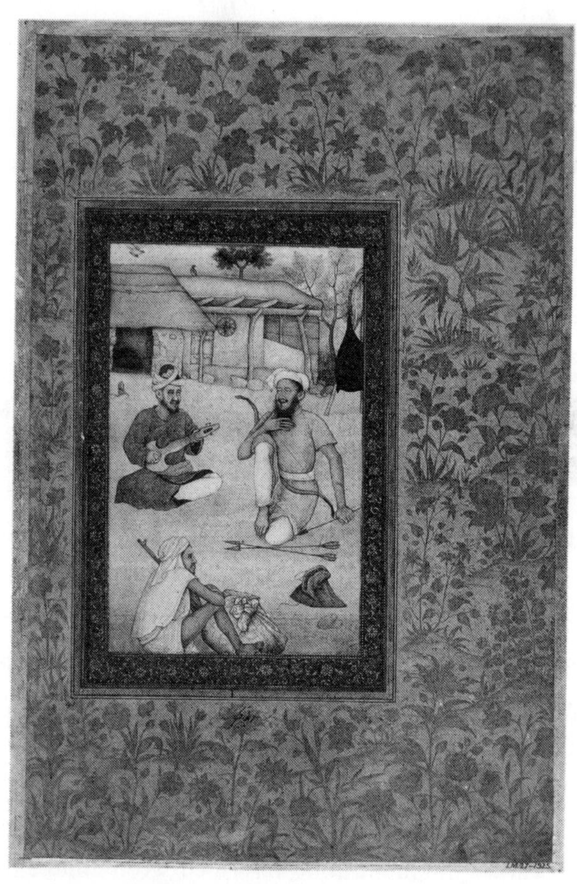

FIGURE 7 *Rubab* player, his companion, and a peasant.
By Bichitr, c. 1615–20. Minto Album, Victoria and Albert
Museum, London (IM, 27 and A-1925).

birds of paradise derived from the paintings of Islamic lands. In the case of European symbols, their use remained strictly confined to adapted pictures or imitations inspired by European examples. However, later, during the seventeenth century under Jahangir and Shah Jahan, European symbols were freely employed in portrait painting to provide a vision emphasizing divinity in the likenesses of the emperor and others. In the context of rendering of symbolic images, Basawan, a prolific painter of Akbar's court, was the foremost. He shows a fascination for European emblematic pictures/figures and exhibited considerable ingenuity in their adaptation by introducing some alterations in consonance with tastes. In the miniature 'Allegorical figure' (c. 1600, MG), ascribed to Basawan, the central figure seems to be an adaptation of the figure of Pietas Regia appearing on the second title page of the first volume of the Antwerp Polyglot Bible (1568–72), presented to Akbar. In this adaptation the Mughal artist has introduced two other kneeling figures and the figure of God the Father holding a long inscribed scroll amidst the clouds. The latter is an exclusively new feature incorporated by the Mughal school. Another unascribed painting, 'Praying Lady' (c. 1600, MG), based on

Basawan's 'Allegorical figure', also depicts God the Father in the same fashion with the difference that a turban is placed on his head.

However, no attempt was ever made at Akbar's atelier to present the emperor as divine; and no divine attributes appear to be linked with Akbar's portraits. The halo and other European symbols, such as cherubs, depicted in some of his portraits are later additions, and these are largely posthumous portraits. During Jahangir's reign various European symbols and motifs, namely cherubs, putti, angels, halo, orbs, and terrestrial globes, were incorporated in Mughal portraits, but the symbolic representation of God in human form is not known to have been attempted. Even so, the last-mentioned theme reappears at Shah Jahan's atelier in a painting executed by Bichitr ('Double portrait of Shah Jahan and Asaf Khan', c. 1645–50, MduL). Here the figure of God the Father is depicted amidst the clouds with an additional feature (not seen in the work of Basawan) of a broad band of light emanating from him, the other end of which converges with the radiating halo around Shah Jahan's head.

The Mughal artist incorporated the symbol of an orb and a terrestrial globe in his work to meet the demand of the emperor's claims or pretensions. Such allegorical portraits symbolized the temporal and spiritual powers of the Mughals.

In the Mughal school the depiction of halo or divine light was restricted only to the image of the emperor. Pictures of holy men and princes adorned with halo are rare exceptions. During Akbar's reign, halo was not used in human portraits. Also, the Mughal artists preferred the European halo for visual representation of their patron. The symbolic form of divine light, the aureole, commonly seen in Islamic paintings (in the representation of prophets), did not attract the attention of the Mughal painters.

The motifs of cherubs emerging from the clouds, holding a European crown, playing musical instruments, and the large golden halo are similar to the European symbols of divinity. The cherubs holding the crown seems to have been derived from the European pictures on the subject, for example, 'Coronation of the Virgin'. These forms and symbols, while expressing the sanctity attached to the man, also hint at exaltation of the dead. It is important to note that Akbar promised immortality to individuals by maintaining records of them in the form of their portraits. He considered portraits to be the 'sign' of an individual passed on to generations to come and, thus, ensuring him immortality.

The placement of the two symbols in a single composition also hinted at symbolism. In this context, an album page containing two portraits, (*a*) 'Jahangir with a halo around his head, holding an orb' (above), and (*b*) 'Youthful Christ holding the Cross' (below), should be considered (Royal Album, CBL, no. 12). These two portraits are ascribed to Hashim and Abu'l Hasan, respectively. The positioning of Jahangir's portrait above the picture of Christ is emblematic and hints at the Mughal artists' way of presenting their master's greatness as being above that of the prophets. Jahangir had his name inscribed even on the forehead of images of Jain Tirthankaras in a few paintings. These instances are symbolic representations of Jahangir's urge for recognition of his suzerainty beyond this world, encompassing religion, belief, and faith. However, as a believer in Islam, he always revered Allah.

In the allegorical picture 'Jahangir embracing Shah Abbas' (FGA, no. 45.9), Abu'l Hasan presents a symbolic depiction of the Mughal emperor's power, prestige, and superiority over the Shah of Iran, the Safavid ruler, who is represented as a humble, weak, and perceptibly smaller figure than that of Jahangir, shown majestically towering over him. The figure of the main subject being made perceptibly larger to emphasize his special status or to attach divinity has long been a tradition in Indian sculpture and painting. The images of the Buddha and Bodhisattvas and the rulers have been shown distinctly larger in size than everyone else in assemblies or groups of men and women in Ajanta paintings. The Mughal painter may not have been aware of it, but he continued to use this classical Indian iconography to symbolize the power and glory of the Mughal emperors and high-ranking nobles.

The symbolism in the Mughal school is not directly connected with the subject of painting but finds its place in the composition due to the spirituality associated with the central subject. Besides, the element of idealism relating to the emblems and signs serves as a link between symbolism and the subject of painting. The relationship between the symbols and the theme/subject of painting is more psychological than functional. The functional part of the symbols is largely in the form of the impression conveyed to the viewer through the visual perception of spirituality, divinity, power, and grandeur; and thus a balance between the organic and ideal worlds is maintained. It also serves as a unifying factor between the earthly and ideally presented forms in a picture plane. The unique characteristic of emblematic Mughal portraits is that the coherence in theme and the elements of unity in presentation are not lost in the picture composition. The emblematic pictures further suggest that the Mughal painters could successfully portray even theological ideas by employing visual symbols, signs, and forms.

It is difficult to ascertain whether the symbols depicted in Mughal pictures were introduced at the instance of the royal patron or whether the artists themselves were attracted to them. However, it seems more plausible that the royal patrons were the force behind them as these symbols were confined to the portrayal of the emperor. The Mughal emperors' general concept of sovereignty infused with divinity gave way to an element of spirituality symbolically attached to their likenesses. Hence, the attachment of the symbols with an individual's portrait seems to have become an artist's mode of visually narrating his supernatural status. The Jesuits' explanation of the Christian images also helped the Mughal artists in more meaningful use of the European symbols.

Jewel Portraits

The beginnings of the jewel portrait can be traced to an inventive idea of Akbar's obliging men who entered his divine order, *Tauhid-i Ilahi*, and started wearing his portrait on their turbans, as a jewel, to commemorate him.

It appears that Jahangir got his father's jewel portrait replaced by his own probably in 1611. Jahangir continued the practice of presenting jewel-portraits to individuals, but in all likelihood as a mark of special royal favour. Sir Thomas Roe, a recipient of the jewel-portrait, writes in 1616:

> I went to visit the King; who as soone as I came in, called to his woemen and reached out a picture of him selfe sett in gould hanging at a wire gould chain, with one pendant foule pearle: which he delivered to Asaph Chan, warning him not to demand any reverence of mee other than such as I would willingly give; …. So Asaph Chan came to mee, and I offered to take it in my hand; but hee made signe to putt of my hatt,

and then putt it about my neck, leading mee right before the king.

Roe goes on to write that the gift of a jewel-portrait was a special favour and the nobles fastened it with a chain on their turbans or wore it as a pendant set with precious stones.

Jahangir is also known to have issued gold presentation *muhr* (so-called portrait-coins) with an impress of his portrait in low-relief. During Shah Jahan's reign the use of jewel-portrait in broches and pendants seems to have become customary, in all likelihood as an adornment.

Equestrian Portraits

Pictures representing an emperor, prince, or a noble as a cavalier are characteristic examples of equestrian portraits which became common during Shah Jahan's reign. It is possible that the Mughal artists were inspired from classical Indian sculpture and painting where equestrian portraits were widely prevalent. Equestrian figures are commonly seen in Ajanta frescoes and a continuity of this form is well represented in Jain and Pala miniatures. The Mughal painters showed ingenuity in adapting this to the times and portraying the best known Persian type of horse in a stylized form. It may be mentioned that the naturalism of depiction was clearly the outcome of European influence.

Genre Scenes

During the seventeenth century, subjects like the visit of the emperor or a prince to an ascetic, roadside performances of musicians, or wandering ascetics, dervishes, and the like, in isolation were frequently painted and here the treatment of the subject probed into the individual's thoughts and feelings. These portraits displayed an unexpected wealth of emotion and insight into the subject's character. It testifies to the development of portraiture into a real genre painting.

The medieval Indian naturalism reached its highest level in Jahangiri paintings. As documentaries and yet as objects of creative painting in medieval India, it was never surpassed. This genre of pictures is clearly more refreshing and natural than the formal and mannered paintings of courtly life.

The portraits of religious men, dervishes, and the like reveal character, which is a special quality of

Mughal portraiture. Human portraits in the Mughal school are not simply chance 'photographs'. In them, artists appear to have aimed at character study, as a consequence of which even the portrayal of the most ordinary men appear so individualized that they figure as real people.

Miniatures that are romantic in tone, or the 'love-scene', constitute another genre depicting the emperor or a prince in the *zenana*, listening to music, and occasionally even in a love scene. The portrayal of amorousness in the Mughal school abounded during the seventeenth century. In such case although the identity of the couple engaged in the act of love is not firmly established, it cannot be ruled out that they are the representatives of the sexual behaviour of the Mughal royalty. However, it is doubtful whether there was a royal sanction to the portrayal of the acts of love of the emperors, princes, and the nobility. The problem arises when we come across pictures on this theme by famous painters of the Mughal school and which even formed part of royal albums. This would suggest, then, that there was a tacit royal sanction to the portrayal of love scenes featuring royalty.

Pictures depicting nudity do not seem to have been favoured at the Mughal atelier, though in the art of Safavid Iran the depiction of nudity was common, especially in love scenes. Mughal pictures on the theme of 'lovelorn lady', of which one composition is ascribed to Kesavdas, are heavily indebted to European sources. European engravings of nude subjects and love-making scenes were familiar to the Mughal artists.

Sensuous pictures in Mughal India were thus sometimes inspired by European examples and these largely flourished outside the imperial atelier. During the mid-seventeenth century, bazaar painters made a business of selling them. The Mughal artists driven to seek a livelihood as commercial freelancers painted pictures with an explicit thrust on sensuality by imitating the works by European artists like Hornthorst. The most favoured theme, 'Hunting by torchlight', depicted semi-nude, leaf-clad aboriginals.

Female Portraits

An observation that Mughal painting is essentially a masculine art is tenable to the extent that there appears no place for portraits of women per se or the portrayal of the various facets of their lives as in the case of men. There always appears a formidable barrier between women and everyday life. However, in numerous sixteenth-century illustrated manuscripts, for example, *Baburnama* (BM; NM), *Ta'rikh-i Khandan-i Timuria* (OPL), *Jami'ut Tawarikh* (IL), and *Akbarnama* (VA; BM & CBL), both royal and ordinary women are depicted as what appears to be in the likeness of an individual. In illustrations of scenes of birth or marriage of a prince seen in the *Ta'rikh-i Khandan-i Timuria* and *Akbarnama*, the faces of women appear to be standardized rather than individualized. In all these paintings women appear true to two types. First, in full profile, as also seen in the illustrations of the *Tutinama* and *Hamzanama* (c. 1560–80), based on the *chaurapanchashikha* style with large fish-shaped eyes, broad cheeks, a distinct chin, and large ear ornaments. The other type, inspired by the Iranian tradition, shows an oval or round face in three-quarters view. These types could serve at best to distinguish Indian and Iranian characters.

The question remains as to why, when female portraits were not aimed at representing actual features, representation of individual women was permitted at all. The explanation appears to lie in Mughal anxiety to depict all the important events in the illustrated manuscripts without loss of any detail. In this quest, ideal portraits were included merely to complete the picture. A caveat relating to the historicity of Mughal portraiture may be entered in relation to the portraits of women, especially queens and princesses. They were certainly painted, as the surviving examples are quite numerous, but the very idealization of the faces and figures shows that they were not drawn from life. This is evident from a portrait supposedly of Nur Jahan, the historicity of which has been urged by O.C. Gangoly and others. Regarding the portrait of Jodha Bai (now at VM, no. 727), Niharranjan Ray (1975) has very pertinent comments to offer. He says that it is a dignified presentation of a princely lady but it is doubtful to what extent it is portraiture in the strict sense of the term in which the Mughal artists and the Mughal court usually denoted it. According to Ray, it appears to be an idealistic interpretation since it is difficult to believe that any male artist would have ever had any chance of setting his eyes on Jodha Bai after her marriage with

Akbar, or as a matter of fact on any lady of the Mughal harem. Indeed, all representations of women in Mughal paintings are of ideal types, not portraits.

Self-portraits

Self-portraiture is not a separate branch of painting. It is in fact essentially a form of portrait painting. However, a curious student of art may be inclined to treat it separately for two reasons. In contrast to portraiture, the artist drawing his own likeness has to work on an unsteady model, usually a mirror reflection. Second, he has a subject with whom he is intimately familiar. A self-portrait is not only the visible self but also the inner self of the artist, a character. It is the last feature that endows the creation with a special charm. Portraits are documents of personalities, characters, and status, which a student of history can ill afford to ignore.

In all probability, self-portraiture was also practised in ancient times. This may be surmised from the numerous literary references, our mainstay in the absence of any specific examples available or cited. Thus, in

Meghdut, Kalidas causes a male character (Love) to address his angered beloved in the following words:

> Whenever, in order to please you, I attempt to portray you in an unpleasant mood on a stone slab with *geru* (Indian red), and myself as lying at your feet (begging pardon) tears well up in my eyes so that tearful eyes are disabled to see. Cruel time cannot bear our meeting even in the picture.

In *Chitralaksana*, Nagnajit narrates the legend of the creation of Indra, Mahadeva, Vishnu, and other gods. We are told how, through the powers bestowed on them by Brahma, they grew into well-proportioned bodies and then painted their own figures.

It would not be stretching the argument to presume, on the basis of this evidence, that ancient Indian painters did paint likenesses of themselves. However, the earliest available specimens of self-portraits are those dating to Akbar's reign. The pictorial colophon of the manuscript *Gulistan* of Sa'di, dated AH 990 (AD 1581), executed by the painter Manohar, represents the portraits of the scribe Muhammad Husain and the painter himself with a book in this hand. This is no mere accident. We frequently find authentic self-portraits of the Mughal painters throughout the sixteenth century and part of the seventeenth. Extant among them are the pictures of Kesavdas dated 1590, two of Daulat executed in 1596 and 1605–9, and of Govardhan dated 1609.

Barrett and Gray as also Asok Kumar Das believe that self-portraiture was not possible at such an early date, that is, AD 1581, in the Mughal school of painting. However, a miniature in the *Khamsa* of Nizami (BM, Or. 12208, AD 1596–7), which represents a princess drawing her own portrait after seeing her image in a mirror held by a maid (folio 206), suggests that this practice must have developed during Akbar's reign. This indicates that self-portraiture was known to the Mughal artist at an early date, contrary to the opposite view. In fact, Manohar's age depicted in the above colophon would probably be 15–17 years, which could be easily contrasted with his age depicted in his other portrait (Gulshan Album, Imperial Library, Gulistan Palace, Tehran, f. 44) executed subsequently in AD 1615–20 by Daulat. It is evident from the style also that the portrait in question was painted during Akbar's reign. Hence the self-portrait of Manohar is not a mere accident at Akbar's court; another example is that of Kesavdas.

It would not be inappropriate to briefly describe the method of self-portrait painting. Folio 206 of the *Khamsa* (above) may be recalled here. The artist portrayed himself after seeing his reflection in a mirror. It is possible that this method may have been in practice in ancient India too. Technically, the mirror will reflect either a front, a three-quarter, or a one-and-a-quarter view, whereas all the self-portraits of the Mughal court painters (with the exception of Daulat's two self-portraits) are in strict profile. It appears that the reflection served as a guide, enabling the artist to draw his profile.

Manohar learnt the art of portrait painting from his father Basawan who excelled in drawing portraits and also other branches of painting. Manohar, whose work belongs to the period 1580–1640, specialized in portraiture. He painted human and animal figures with remarkable success.

Manohar's portrait is a profile which is a character-istic feature of the eastern India school. This particular form of painting seems to have acted as a trendsetter. Subsequently, the early Mughal style, where the three-quarter face was the rule, began to be increasingly replaced by the native tradition until the latter fell into disuse by the first quarter of the seventeenth century. Indeed, throughout this period, portraiture generally imbibed the native style.

The self-portrait of Kesavdas, with a scroll of paper in hand, next to Manohar, appears in the foreground of a miniature (Jahangir Album, State Museum, Berlin f. 25a). An inscription in Devanagari on the scroll reads: *Siddhi Sri Jalaldin Patishahi chiranjeev. Samvat 1646 Paush sudi naumi likhitam Kesavdas, chitrakar* (Long live His Highness Jalaluddin Akbar Padishah. Samvat 1646 [AD 1590] on the 9th of the lighted half of Pausha. Written by Kesavdas, the painter).

Chronogically, the third self-portrait (of Daulat) is a part of the pictorial colophon (folio 325) of the manuscript *Khamsa* (above). The colophon, written on the 24th day of the month of Azar, Akbar's 40th regnal year (AD 1596–7), was illustrated later during Jahangir's time. According to an inscription on the wall panel just below the niches, the colophon was painted at the command of Jahangir. The date of the painting is partly erased, but it may safely be put as AD 1609–10, that is, Jahangir's 4th regnal year. The inscription reads: *Allah-o Akbar. Ba hukm-i Shah Jahangir naqsh-i in taswir namud banda-i Daulat shabih-i khwud. San chahar (?)*

[julus] san 101 (8) raqam kamtarin faqir al haqir Daulat (God is great. This painting is illuminated at the order of the Emperor Jahangir. Imperial servant did paint his likeness [in] fourth regnal year, AH 101 [8] [that is, AD 1609–10]. Work of most humble Daulat). There is another inscription on the left folio of the book placed before that of the scribe. It reads: *'Amal-i banda-i dargah Daulat* (Work of the imperial servant Daulat). Daulat was a *khanazad* (imperial house-born) according to the inscriptions on the miniatures executed by him in *Baburnama*, and in a miniature on folio 148 in the Gulshan Album (above).

Another self-portrait of Daulat appears in a margin-painting on folio 44 in the Gulshan Album. The folio painted by Daulat contains portraits of artists, including Abu'l Hasan, Bishandas, Govardhan, Manohar, and Daulat himself. According to the inscription on the sheet shown as held by Daulat in his left hand, these portraits were painted at Jahangir's command. The inscription reads: *Allah-o Akbar. Ba hukm-i Shah Jahangir naqsh-i in taswir namud, Banda-i daulat-shabih-i khwud. Tahrir qaila wa raqima faqir al-haqir Daulat* (God is great. This painting is illuminated at the order of the Emperor Jahangir. Imperial servant did paint his likeness. Work of the most humble Daulat). A distinct resemblance in the features of these self-portraits shows Daulat's skill in portraiture.

Govardhan's self-portrait, like Daulat's second self-portrait, appears on the margin-painting on folio 25b in the Jahangir Album (State Library, Berlin). Kuhnel and Goetz (1926) have described this portrait. The inscription given on the folios of the book placed before the artist reads: *'Amal-i kamtarin-i khanazadan Govardhan, Jahangir Shahi, wald Bhawanidas, khatm shud san 1018* (Work of the meanest Imperial house-born, Govardhan, the servant of Jahangir, the son of Bhawanidas, finished in the year AH 1018/AD 1609–10). It shows that Govardhan was a khanazad. In this portrait he appears to be a youth of 18-20, and it bears close resemblance to the portrait of this painter executed by Daulat.

Self-portraits known from Shah Jahan's atelier are found in the *Padshahnama* (Royal Library, Windsor, no. 773, c. 1635–40). It contains the self-portraits of Balchand, Mirar, and Payag. Balchand's self-portrait is on folio 43, 'Jahangir bids farewell to Khurram, departing for his campaign against Rana of Mewar in 1614 (c. 1635)'. Here Balchand has portrayed himself in the extreme corner (below) holding a small rectangular sheet of paper.

The double-page illustration in the same manuscript, 'Khurram on his return after the reduction of Rana Amar Singh, embraced by Jahangir', c. 1640, contains the self-portrait of Mirar on the extreme bottom corner (folio 49). The pose of the artist with an inscribed sheet of paper in his hand and the positioning of the figure in the corner are the same as in Balchand's self-portrait (folio 43). The inscription given on the sheet is 'Mirar'.

Payag's self-portrait is also to be found in the same manuscript on folio 195 among the group of courtiers on the extreme right hand corner of the miniature (c. 1640). It also represents the artist holding a rectangular sheet of paper in his right hand with the inscription on it. It reads: *Allah-o Akbar. Raqam Payag, biradar-i Balchand* (God is Great. Work of Payag, brother of Balchand). M.C. Beach has identified this Payag with the Payag of Akbar's atelier who worked on the folios of *Baburnama* (c. 1600). However, the age depicted in this portrait, about 30–5, does not support this view. In all likelihood, Payag of Shah Jahan's court and Payag of Akbar's court were two different individuals.

Beach has also identified the bearded figure shown on the extreme right-hand corner in the miniature 'Jahangir proffering a sufi' (FGA, no. 42.15), painted by Bichitr, as a self-portrait of the artist. However, this was first suggested by Ettinghausen, but without offering any evidence. Here, the figure is shown holding a sheet of paper identical in size and shape to those depicted in the self-portraits of Balchand, Mirar, and Payag, with the difference of an unsigned miniature on it. As it bears no inscription, identification of the figure as the self-portrait of Bichitr remains doubtful. Das has identified this figure with Ibrahim Adil Shah.

Das has further noticed a self-portrait of Farrukh Beg (Sotheby Sale Catalogue, 28 March 1983, lot 5). The inscription on it reads: *Shabih wa 'amal-i Farrukh Beg musauwir* (Portrait and painting by Farrukh Beg musauwir). Losty (1982) has also suggested the figure of an artist shown at work in an illustration in the *Masnavi* of Zafar Khan (RAS, MS Persian 310, folios 19–20), as the self-portrait of Bishandas, but this is quite unconvincing. The miniature is an unascribed piece and the identity of the painter is not known.

Self-portraits are pictorial records of the artists' appearance, personality, and their sartorial taste. They are very valuable in the absence of textual evidence about the artists in the chronicles. These pictorial representations sometimes also help us in ascertaining their methods of painting, the material they used, and their achievement at a certain stage in their lives. Their age indicated in the portraits also help us to determine the length of their stay at the atelier.

Nevertheless, self-portraits as a source material related to the history of the common people, which remains largely untold, has limitations. A significant development in sixteenth- and seventeenth-century Indian art, self-portraiture was a contribution of Mughal court painters. However, it never became a popular art form and only a handful of painters are known to have painted their own portraits. Also, till the mid-eighteenth century, self-portraiture is conspicuously absent in Indian art.

4

Depictions of Natural History

Birds and Animals

Zoological study is a significant aspect of Mughal painting. After portraiture, the most famous genre is the picturization of birds, animals, and plants in blossom. Numerous representations of animals and birds painted separately or in groups in the scenes of hunting, bird-trappings, animal-fights, and the like, are examples of vivid, minutely detailed, and realistic Mughal art. These paintings demonstrate the Mughal painters' unparalled originality, objectivity, and naturalism. The abundance of such illustrations of birds, animals, plants, and flowers during the sixteenth and seventeenth centuries reflects the Mughal emperors' passion for nature and wildlife.

The keen interest shown by the Mughal emperors in the study of flora and fauna gave the artists a special impetus to portray nature and wildlife, a phenomenon never witnessed earlier in Indian art. Babur, the founder of the Mughal empire and a great naturalist, gave a detailed description of birds, animals, flowers, and trees in India in his memoirs. His precise observations served as a basis for the representation of birds and animals in drawings.

Jahangir's curiosity in natural history was more intense and he wanted to see greater likeness in the representations of wildlife. His enthusiasm for knowledge of natural history was further sharpened by his scientific curiosity, which led to a specialization in art and a precision in drawing the exact likeness of the living creatures in line and colour. Most exclusive pictures of wildlife executed under Jahangir's patronage clearly show that the Mughal school owes its highest achievement to this emperor. The continuity of this tradition is well maintained in a large number of bird, animal, and flower studies done during the post-Jahangir period.

Another factor responsible for the interest of the painters in wildlife was probably the fact that they were called upon to paint animals and birds for illustrating fables and legends like the *Tutinama, Anwar-i Suhaili, 'Iyar-i Danish,* and *'Aja'ib-al Makhluqat* at Akbar's court. Subsequently, the Mughal painters became well familiar with the character and behaviour of the birds and animals. This familiarity gave an extra dimension to the paintings. Thus, the illustrations did not remain confined to mere depictions of the physical features. They also became warm and sincere depictions of the moods, habits, and emotions of the birds and animals. In illustrating the legends involving animal characters, painters not only adopted a direct approach to the subject but also exercised some amount of freedom and imagination.

Baburnama miniatures (c. 1595–1600) are the earliest depictions of natural history. It contains 120 illustrations of the flora and fauna of India, which closely follow the descriptions. The animals are generally drawn either in pairs or groups or in singles, but in compositional scenes of hunting or bird-trapping they are clustered together. The emphasis on the exact delineation of the individual character of the subject is noticeable in these miniatures. One cannot fail to admire the presence of minute details; nothing eludes the artist's eye, whether it is the texture of hair, or peculiarities of horns and ears, mane and tail, or fur and plumage. They are so realistically depicted and disinguished that each species is clearly individualized and separated from the others.

The naturalistic treatment of birds and animals becomes more and more apparent by the close of Akbar's reign. The purely linear, pictorial, and decorative representation of the Persian school was abandoned at this juncture. Sympathy coupled with scientific orientation to the study of animals in the paintings seems to be the cause of such transition. The sympathetic attitude for the animals incidentally was in line with the pre-Mughal Indian tradition. The only difference was that the purpose of the Mughal artists was to do justice to naturalistic portraiture and, hence, they were not required to inspire adoration and reverence.

The miniature 'Akbar mounted on an elephant crossing a bridge of boats in pursuit of another elephant' (Akb, VA, IS, 2-1896, no. 117/22-3) by the great masters Basawan and Chetar depicts figures of thundering elephants and is imbued with intense physical action. It is one of the most sensational illustrations, capturing with great realism the powerful movements of the animals. Mention has to be made of a remarkable painting by Miskin, 'Buffaloes in combat' (MMA, no. 1988. 258), which surpassed Basawan's work, capturing the violent confrontation in a very expressive and vivid manner. The background is treated in the flat, screen-like Persian style, further isolating and emphasizing the ponderous fury of the animals.

During Akbar's era a distinct *qalam* had come into existence, but specialization in various branches of art had to wait till Jahangir's advent on the firmament of royal art patronage. Manohar and Mansur from Akbar's atelier were recognized as the two most distinguished specialists in painting animal portraits in the succeeding era (see Figure 8). They were found compatible with Jahangir's measures of excellence.

Jahangir added to the existing importance of the art of painting by treating it as a major source of historical documentation of events:

Although King Babur has described in his Memoirs the appearance and shapes of several animals, he had never ordered the painters to make pictures of them. As these animals appeared to me to be very strange, I both described them and ordered the painters should draw them in the *Jahangir-nama*, so that the amazement that arose from hearing of them might be increased.

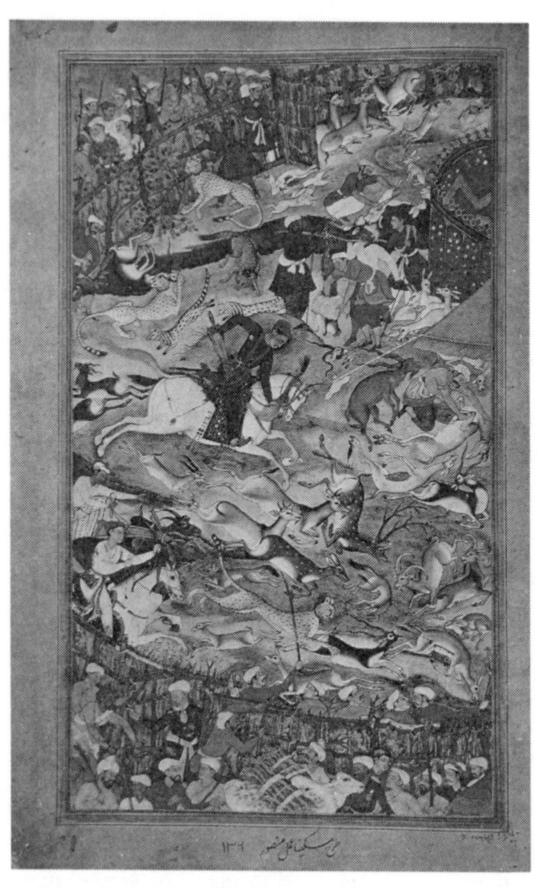

FIGURE 8   Akbar hunts near Lahore in 1567. By Miskin and Mansur. Illustration to the *Akbarnama*, c. 1590–5. Victoria and Albert Museum, London (IS 2–1896 56/117).

References to the portrayal of bird and animal pictures at the command of the emperor found in the *Tuzuk-i Jahangiri* further affirm Jahangir's attitude towards this branch of painting.

Jahangir was always concerned about accuracy and naturalism in portrait painting of both men and animals. An interesting event, which also throws light on Mansur's career, took place when he was accompanying the emperor's retinue to Kashmir (dated 1620). He not only painted more than a hundred varieties of flowers blossoming in that exotic valley, but also painted a picture of a bird called *saj* (dipper), seen at Sukh Nag, at the emperor's bidding. Jahangir records:

In this stream I saw a bird like a *saj*. A *saj* is of black colour and has white spots, while this bird is of the same colour as a *bulbul* with white spots, and it dives and remains for a long time underneath, and then comes up from a different place. I ordered them to catch and bring two or three of these birds, that I might ascertain whether they are waterfowl and were web-footed, or had open feet like land birds. They caught two and brought them. One died immediately, and the other lived for a day. Its feet were not webbed like a duck's. I ordered *Nadir-ul-'Asr* Ustad Mansur to draw its likeness.

A picture of this bird ascribed to Mansur is available at the Kevorkian Album (MMA, 55.1210.16r).

Jahangir's scientific curiosity and innate desire for documentation of rarities gave a tremendous impetus to zoological portraits of immense value and quality. Among the contemporaries of Mansur who also portrayed wildlife at Jahangir's atelier were Abu'l Hasan, Farrukh Beg, Govardhan, 'Inayat, Manohar, Muhammad Nadir, Murad (or Mirar), and Pidarath. However, the total number of animal paintings ascribed to these artists is far less than what Mansur alone painted. Mansur's towering command in this branch of painting can be judged from the fact that Jahangir could trust no one else more than him for doing bird and animal paintings. This is an indisputable proof of Mansur being the leading exponent of natural history painting at Jahangir's atelier. He became one of the top luminaries of the Mughal atelier which directly functioned under the emperor's guidelines or instructions. Mansur achieved permanence and relevance both for his creativity and naturalism, a naturalism that could be the pride of zoological museums and art collections, with equal grace. His true lifelike masterpieces of individual animals are so lively that they captured moments of the eternal flow of life in nature and simultaneously became palimpsests of those species of nature, relevant to all times.

The miniatures showing a groom leading a blackbuck (c. 1615–20, CW, VA, IM, no. 134-1921), one of the few animal pictures ascribed to Manohar—a prolific painter at Jahangir's court—is one of the finest genre pictures of the Mughal school (see Figure 9). It is a magnificent study of animal life which is perfect in characterization and technique. It also beautifully depicts the coaxing attitude and expression of the keeper, as if trying to overcome the hesitation of his well-trained pet. Another composition by this artist is equally important as it establishes him as a clever painter of horses (Johnson Album, IOL, v. 3, no. 1). Although this painting is much damaged, the drawing bears evidence of a skilled artist who had studied the animal very carefully and had a great knowledge of horses.

Zoological portraits representing birds and animals are the most intimate and faithful studies. In these paintings the figures dominate the whole composition,

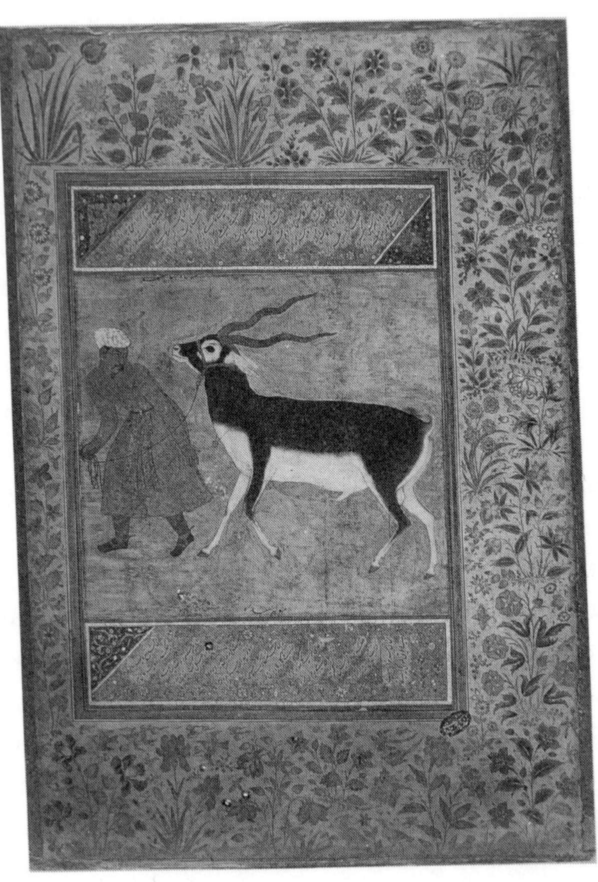

FIGURE 9   A blackbuck being led by its keeper. By
Manohar, c. 1610–15. Bequeathed by Lady Wantage.
Victoria and Albert Museum, London (IM, 134–1921).

set against a subdued background. These pictures generally display simpler composition accommodating the central theme more spaciously, probably to allow maximum detail. While there are drawings filled with spirited movement and violent action, the best studies are the portraits of single animals or pairs. It is not the action but the technical finesse presented with refined workmanship in a rather restrained manner that makes the pictures valuable. Exotic and uncommon birds, animals, plants, and flowers from medieval times become real. The Mughal portraits are an outcome of slow careful work imbued with realism, achieved within the framework of the traditional manner of draughtsmanship. The Mughal painter never followed the Persian mode of depicting birds and animals which was purely linear and descriptive, but instead always aimed at portraying the animal as an 'individual' with an emphasis on physiognomy.

Accuracy achieved by well-defined outlines and rendering of maximum detail is the chief characteristic of Mughal studies of wildlife. Attention was given to the use of pigments reflecting the actual colour of the subject. One cannot fail to admire the minute observation of the artists who so realistically depicted the characteristic physical features of the various birds and animals—hair, horns, ears, tail, fur, or plumage—that one can identify the species at first glance itself. The artists painted them after careful study, examining the object closely and several times, as their creations were not merely a copy of the external appearance of the animals but objective illustrations of their mood as well. The depiction of birds and animals in their natural surroundings further enhances the lively effect.

It is important to note that the realism in the Mughal painters' work is confined to the artists' visual experience. This element of art is apparent in Mughal painting from the very beginning. One can observe a shift from the strict conventions of Persian art in the depiction of the animal figures represented in the miniatures of the *Anwar-i Suhaili* (dated 1570, SOAS). These are more natural and self-possessed than the remote and exquisite animals of the Persian school and appear more deeply engaged by their action. In fact, with the general emergence of Indian ideals, the Persian traditions in Mughal art became weak and it facilitated a more naturalistic rendering of birds and animals. Also, the patron's interest in realistic-cum-ornithological portrait studies does not find a parallel in the art of Persia or even pre-Mughal India.

The quality of lively naturalism achieved by the Mughal painters was accentuated through the influence of European techniques of painting. The European influence is evident in the drawings of birds and animals only in context of the deep shading and heavy modelling occasionally employed to highlight the contours and various parts of the body.

Flowering Plants

Mughal art pioneered the use and representation of plants in full blossom in painting. While flowers were a common motif and an integral past of design in Indian art from early times, it was only with the emergence of the Mughal school that they became main subjects of paintings rather than embellishments. However, this started from the seventeenth century onwards.

The development of this genre at the Mughal school is to be understood against the backdrop of the Mughal emperors' interest in nature. Babur has given a graphic description of the flowers of India in his memoirs. His description containing botanical details is indeed remarkable. Of *kaner* (*Nerium odorum*, the oleander) he writes:

> It grows both red and white. Like the peach–flower, it is five petalled. It is like the peach-bloom, but opens 14 or 15 flowers from one place, so that seen from a distance, they look like one great flower. The oleander-bush is taller than the rose-bush. The red oleander has a sort of scent, faint and agreeable. It also blooms well and profusely in the rains, and it also grows through most of the year.

About *kiura* (*Pandanus odoratissimus*, the screwpine) he notices:

> It has a very agreeable perfume. Musk has the defect of being dry; this may be called moist musk—a very agreeable perfume. The tree's singular appearance notwithstanding, it has flowers perhaps 1½ to 2 *qarish* [13½ to 18 inches] long. It has long leaves having the character of the reed *gharau* and having spines. Of these leaves, while pressed together bud-like, the outer ones are the greener and more spiny; the inner ones are soft and white. In amongst these inner leaves grow things like what belongs to the middle of a flower, and from these things comes the excellent perfume. When

the tree first comes up not yet showing any trunk, it is like the bush (*buta*) of the male-reed, but with wider and more spiny leaves. What serves it for a trunk is very shapeless, its roots remaining shewn.

Actual portraits executed towards the end of the sixteenth century by the painters of Akbar's atelier are available in the various manuscripts of the *Baburnama*.

Babur's description of the panoramic view of blossoms during spring in Sindh once again testifies to his being a connoisseur of flowers:

In some places sheets of yellow flowers bloomed in plots; in others sheets of red flowers in plots, in some red and yellow bloomed together. We sat on a mound near the camp to enjoy the sight. There were flowers on all sides of the mound, yellow here, red there, as if arranged regularly to form a sextuple. On two sides there were fewer flowers but as far as the eye reached, flowers were in bloom. In spring near Parashawar the field of flowers are very beautiful indeed (account of the year AH 925/AD 1519).

Jahangir's innate love for nature received fuller expression during his visit to Kashmir in 1620, when his excitement on seeing the valley of flowers knew no bounds. He writes: 'It was broad, and plain after plain, and mead after mead, of flowers. Sweet-smelling plants of narcissus, violet, and strange flowers that grow in this country, came to view.... The flowers of Kashmir are beyond counting and calculation'. He provides a graphic description of the beauty of flowers:

Kashmir is a garden of eternal spring, or an iron fort to a palace of kings—a delightful flower-bed, and a heart-expanding heritage for dervishes.... The red rose, the violet, and the narcissus grew of themselves; in the fields, there are all kinds of flowers and all sorts of sweet-scented herbs more than can be calculated. In the soul-enchanting spring the hills and plains are filled with blossoms; the gates, the walls, the courts, the roofs, are lighted up by torches of banquet-adorning tulips. What shall we say of these things or of the wide meadows (*julgaha*) and the fragrant trefoil?

He subsequently describes a number of flowers of Kashmir valley and puts on record: 'The flowers that are seen in the territories of Kashmir are beyond all calculation. Those that *Nadir-u'l 'Asr Ustad* Mansur has painted are more than hundred.'

Although Jahangir mentions more than a hundred flower paintings of Mansur, only four are extant. 'Tulip' (c. 1621) and 'Iris' (c. 1621) are among the best flower paintings known from Mansur's brush in the Habibganj Collection (HC) and the Nasiruddin Album (IL). His extraordinary achievement in floral painting is evident in the study of the tulip (see Figure 10). The detailing in the lifelike representation can be seen under a magnifying glass: the bends of the stems, the drawing of the leaves, the stages of flowering (from bud to full blossom, shown from different angles), a close-up of the pollen grains at the end of the stamens (six in number), and the delicate venation (in a few leaves) proceeding towards the margin of the leaf blade in a more or less parallel direction (convergent type)—a characteristic of lanceolate leaves of the plants of the lily family (Liliaceae). It seems that the species chosen by Mansur is *Tulipa clusiana*.

The butterfly and dragonfly (?) shown hovering above the tulip flowers are in consonance with Mansur's thrust towards imparting realism in his studies. There is an attempt not only to suggest the skyline but also to intensify the naturalistic impact of the flower study through the addition of ecological harmony that exists

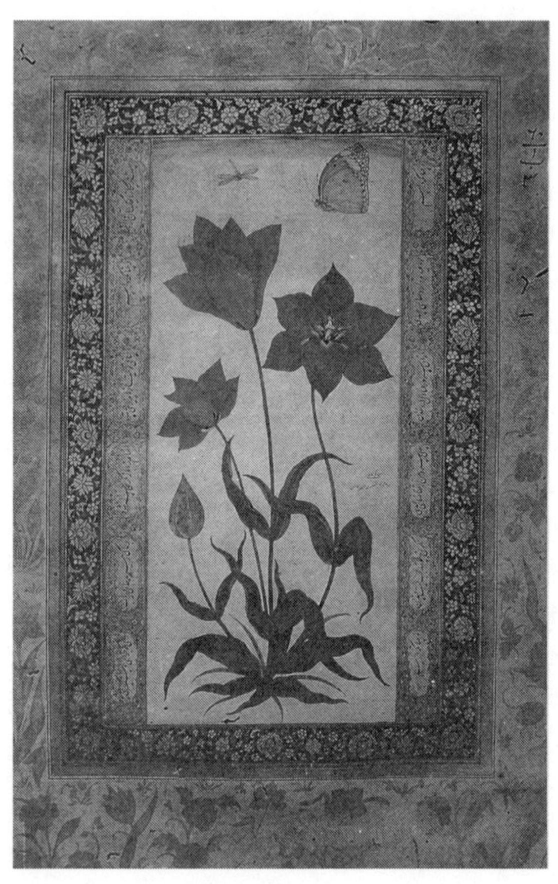

FIGURE 10 Tulip and butterfly. By *Nadir-u'l Asr* Mansur, c. 1620–1. Habibganj Collection, Aligarh Muslim University (60-1-B [3]).

in nature. The very pale background does help in brightening up in relief the flowering plant and also enhances with ease its vertical movement without having to concentrate much on spacing the sky as one might expect otherwise. Also, the dense clustering of the leaves at the base has a deliberate purpose and design: it suggests the plant being rooted in the soil. In its upward growth the leaves have a light openness balanced by a bud and there is a focus on the different folds of petals concerting with various stages of blossoming of the flower. At every stage of drawing, Mansur has deftly avoided monotony. It is a remarkable example of the delicacy required in realistic flower drawing as well as in the control of space.

Another well-known flower painting is that of the iris. This study shares some common compositional elements with the tulip, including the hovering of an insect over the blossom, the approaching bird, and flowers projecting different facets at different angles. Together they reveal the total cross section of the flower. It conforms to the rules of naturalistic study without losing its aesthetic appeal.

In such paintings, in order to enliven the surroundings, capture rhythm of movement, and manage the compositional aspects, Mansur prefers to depict birds, butterflies, and other insects hovering over the blossoms. This style of Mansur influenced the works of other painters as well. One could see a similar approach in the work of Muhammad Nadir's 'Yellow narcissus' (c. 1620–25), in the Cowasji Jehangir Collection (CSM). Here also, the plant is depicted against a subdued flat background, a characteristic trait of Mughal portrait painting followed in studies of flowers. The butterfly, while characteristic, appears as an aid to the natural surroundings.

A large number of Mughal flower paintings in the Dara Shukoh Album (IOL), 19 in all, though not always naturalistic and often derived from the European model, establish the continuity of the flower painting genre after Jahangir.

The Mughal painter also used flowering plants to decorate broad margins surrounding miniatures and pages of calligraphy. Careful studies of flowering plants with botanical details, identified as narcissus, dianthus, iris, tulip, poppy, dahlia, rose, chrysanthemum, crocus, morning glory, and primula, appear as margin decorations.

5

Border Decoration

The border (*hashiya*) is a secondary part of painting (*taswir*). Nevertheless, the Mughal artists regarded it a necessary element. Its primary function was to regularize the outlines or margins of the painting and give it an artistic finish. The artist enjoyed considerable liberty, and within the narrow strips of the border, he tried to display all that he could in order to provide the painting with additional décor. He could choose contrasting motifs or colours to emphasize the main theme or enhance its aesthetic appeal by rendering it in matching colours and objects, such as creepers, flowering plants, wildlife, and various designs like arabesques and geometrical motifs. The practice reflects the fondness of the painter and his patron for ornamentation.

Margin painting developed in the last quarter of the sixteenth century at the Mughal school and became an integral part of the one-page miniatures or album pictures in vogue at the beginning of the seventeenth century. It is generally accepted that margin decoration was so deeply associated with Mughal painting during the seventeenth century that no miniature was considered complete unless it was surrounded by a highly ornamented border. Illuminated borders appear to differ in purpose for book-illustrations and album paintings, though their basic decorative nature remains intact.

In the earliest Indian illustrated manuscripts, that is of eastern India or Pala school (800–1200), border-painting is not in evidence. This is equally true of Jain paintings from western India or Gujarat school of 1200–1400. Nevertheless, ornamentation appears in the vertical narrow columns between two adjacent illustrations or in vertical panels within the text. Generally stylized floral motifs, geometrical forms, and mythological signs appear to have been used in border decoration in a variety of ways. A change is, however, seen in the western India school during the fifteenth century (after 1450) under the impact of Persian art. The use of bright colours, gold pigment, and minute details in the illustrations were the principal charac-teristics of Persian art acquired by the artists of this school. The illuminated margins of the manuscripts *Kalpasutra* and *Kalkacharya Katha* (c. 1475, Devasano Pado Bhandar, Ahmedabad), adopted from Persian examples, are rare instances of this Persian influence on western Indian art. These depict floral meanders, scrolls, and cartouches with figures of female dancers, warriors, angels, birds, and animals, arabesques, mythi-cal creatures, and a variety of trees, all imbibing Persian traits. However, such border decorations never became popular in Indian manuscript painting. Further, their continuity is not traceable in the western India school or any other centres of painting in pre-Mughal India.

In classical manuscript painting, the traditional arrangement was to surround the miniatures with two or three narrow bands of straight lines. This method remained in vogue and continued to be practised at the Rajasthani, Mughal, and Deccan centres of paint-ing. In the early Mughal miniatures there appear four to eight or even more narrow bands in black, deep-green, blue, white, and gold pigments. Lines are drawn with accurate measurement of length and breadth. These are termed *jadwal* or *khat*. A very narrow space is left between two lines. It is sometimes painted with gold pigment. In cases when the space is broader, it is decorated with floral design, called *bel*. Deep and contrasting pigments are preferred. The earliest example of this are the illuminated margins of the *Diwan-i Hafiz*, c. 1582–85 (RRL).

The Mughal artist was inspired by Persian art (especially the Timurid and Safavid schools) where margin painting had developed since the early fifteenth century. In Islamic art, illumination of the margins developed along with manuscript painting. The earliest examples are the margins illuminated in gold, representing panels of decorative rosettes, mostly used to decorate the pages of the Holy Qur'an during the tenth and eleventh centuries. The convention of margin decoration held a distinguished place in the Sasanid art of Persia in AD 1200 where margin decoration developed in its unique form, including abstract patterns, highly stylized palmettes, and floral arabesques. Margin painting also flourished at Tabriz in AD 1400. This trend continued in Timurid art (especially at the Shiraz school) and later at Herat and the Safavid centres of painting in 1600. At these centres, arabesques in gold were widely practised, and in addition, broad margins with decorative designs or with depictions of animate figures as well as fabulous birds and animals set within landscapes were common. Gold painting for borders, which was introduced during the Timurid period in AD 1500, rapidly spread from Bukhara to other centres of painting in Persia and subsequently to India.

Illuminated border decoration was not prevalent during the early stages of Mughal painting. Miniatures of the *Hamzanama* (c. 1562–80), *Anwar-i Suhaili* (AD 1570, SOAS), and *Tutinama* (c. 1570–80, CMA; CBL) show the bands of ruled lines immediately surrounding the picture in a variety of colours. The margin illumination in the *Tutinama*, one of the earliest Mughal manuscripts, in gold dust is similar in technique already in vogue in fifteenth-century Persia, in both decorative art and painting. In this method fine gold power is sprinkled, thinly coated, or applied with a pounce bag.

Illustrated margin appears in the Mughal school only after 1580. Examples of this are the margins of the miniatures executed in the manuscripts *Diwan-i Hafiz* (AD 1582, CBL), *Diwan* of Anwari (AD 1588, FAM), *Baharistan* of Jami (AD 1595, BLO), *Khamsa* of Amir Khusrau (AD 1597–8, WAG), and *Khamsa* of Nizami (AD 1597–8, BM). In these examples, the subject and the technique of margin illumination are directly derived from the Safavid and Timurid traditions of fifteenth and sixteenth centuries. Here an execution of forms exclusively in gold pigments is the most favoured method. In these motifs the mythical figures (like winged-lion, dragon, the *simurgh*, monsters biting and chewing) against a rocky landscape and the execution of forms in gold against a beige ground are Persian traits directly adopted by the Mughal artists.

An original expansion of the theme of border decoration is seen in the margins executed during the seventeenth century. The broad margins in this period portrayed amidst landscape, floral scrolls or arabesques, hunting scenes, a variety of artisans and professionals, portraits of the emperor, nobles, saints, artists, and ordinary men. The arabesques now appeared more closely designed and thematically the margin painting became more comprehensive with the incorporation of figures adapted from the European engravings and prints. In addition, the naturalistic flower plant motifs painted in the wide margins at Jahangir's studio exemplified a new undertaking in border painting which were all characteristically Mughal in origin. In the Safavid painting of the mid-seventeenth century, however, wide margins filled with plants with blossoms were executed in gold on pink ground.

Margin painting with a double picture frame, that is, an inner margin (narrow) and an outer margin (broad), appeared during the seventeenth century. The inner margin is largely embellished with stylized floral motifs, scrolling gold palmettes and floral forms, and fanciful interwining leaves set in running pattern painted in gold or bright pigment on deep-coloured background, generally Persian blue. A variation is noticeable too in the decoration of the inner margin while it accommodated panels of calligraphy. The verses, which are well calligraphed, often bear no relation to the theme of the picture in the centre. Their arrangement in tablets were based on Safavid and Timurid traditions. In addition to this decorative narrow band, there is the broad margin. Richly elaborated broad margins freely accommodated flowering plant motifs, bird and animal figures amidst the foliage, human figures, and the like, besides floral arabesques and stylized patterns. However, a Mughal artist preferred naturalistic portrayal of objects and his studies took the form of portrait studies. In the motifs of the flower plants, the pattern of the leaves spreads out from the base of the plant. The drawings, treated as nature studies, are very fine and detailed. The plants are identifiable. In an embellished form the plants with blossoms are executed in gold on a pink or a deep blue or a buff ground (see Figures 11 and 12). The careful studies of flower plants containing botanical details include the narcissus, dianthus, iris, tulip, poppy, dahlia, rose, chrysanthemum, peonies, marigold, corcus, morning glory, and premula. The special focus on naturalistic depiction of flowers employed in the decorative border schemes during Jahangir's reign might have been due to the Mughal painters' visit to the Kashmir valley. Mansur's flower paintings could also have induced the rise of this genre.

Most sumptuous margins from the Mughal school, characteristic of Jahangir's period, are the borders decorated with birds and animals amidst fantastic foliage. In these instances, sparsely set figures of birds painted in bright colours appear amidst the plants and trees executed in varying shades of gold pigment. It is notable that the drawings of birds are very realistic and are indeed actual representations of their species.

Another distinctive feature of the Mughal margins is that they depicted human figures. The most

FIGURE 11   Margin decoration derived from a miniature by Sahifa Banu. Bequeathed by Lady Wantage. Victoria and Albert Museum, London (IM, 117-A-1921).

distinguished examples of such paintings are from the Gulshan Album (Gulistan Palace, Imperial Library, Tehran); Jahangir Album (Staatsbibliothek, Berlin; Freer Gallery or Art, Washington), and Royal Albums (Chester Beatty Library, Dublin). The margin painting on a folio from the Jahangir Album shows craftsmen and professionals engaged in 'book-production' (Freer Gallery of Art, Washington, D.C., dated c. 1610, no. 54.116). It represents six men at work. They are shown (anti-clockwise) polishing a sheet with a burnisher, binding the manuscript, filing the edges of a bound volume, making a wooden book-stand (*rehal*), smelting gold, and finally the scribe writing in a bound volume. The tools and implements used by the book-binders, carpenters, goldsmith, and the scribe, vividly shown in the margin painting, are a source for the study of the technology of the period. It also testifies to artists' direct observation of the subject. The figures are set in a conventional manner amidst a landscape of hillocks, bushes, and plants with blossoms painted in gold against a beige ground. The details of costumes and other objects including tools and implements are highlighted with polychrome washes which too have delicate golden tones. In another example from the same collection, the theme of the border decoration illustrating six figures (c. 1610) including a scribe, a prince, and handworkers interspersed amidst rocks and bushes is similarly treated. These are the examples where an artist has enjoyed greater measure of freedom of expression. In this context the margin painting containing the portraits of the artists Abu'l Hasan, Bishandas, Govardhan, Manohar, and Daulat (self-portrait) known in the Gulshan Album (IL) is of considerable significance as it shows rare portraits of the Mughal artists. The method of execution of details in drawing is very much similar to the examples above. The portraits are executed in tones of gold with the application of colours and tints for the faces, costumes, and highlights. Margins ascribed to the master painters Aqa Riza, Balchand, Bishandas, Daulat, Govardhan, and others show that during the seventeenth century margin decoration with figural drawings had become important. The human figures in them seem to have been painted with direct and penetrating observation. The marvelous small portraits rendered in colour or tints are thus recognizable and are contemporary visual references to these men.

European themes, derived from Flemish and German prints, too, fascinated the Mughal painters who not only imitated and adapted them, but also superimposed them upon a conventional landscape background in a wide border. In the broad margins of the album pictures preserved in Jahangir Album (Berlin), virtually identical versions of several well-known European subjects executed by Albert Durer and others appear to have been included. In them, adapted versions of the figures taken from Durer's works, for example, 'Virgin under the tree', 'St Peter', and 'St John', appear interspersed in the fantastic rocky landscape. Further, an adapted version based on Durer's work 'Figure of St John', earlier executed by Abu'l Hasan in 1601, appears again in the border decoration of the Jahangir Album. Besides, numerous European subjects, Christian themes and also autochthonous subjects, exact sources of which are not known, too, are freely accommodated in border decoration. A spacious margin painting from the Jahangir Album (FGA, No. 56.12) shows grouping of religious and mythological subjects copied from the European engravings/prints. It represents God the Father floating in space, a female and a child with tablets (theme identified by its inscription 'Geometria'), a Christian saint (possibly St Anthony), the Ship of Salvation with the Christ child, and finally the Virgin holding the Christ child and the infant St John amidst the conventional landscape with hills, trees, and plants executed in gold against a beige ground. In another example, a margin painting from the same collection shows five European women: one holding a painting representing a saint, and another in praying position prostrates before the picture. One woman on the left margin is shown with an open book in her hand. Two other women are shown at the bottom on either side of an infant child. In such examples, the treatment of the figures adapted from the European examples is thoroughly in association with Renaissance art, whereas the landscape background is invariably akin to the Mughal style.

Margins decorated with conventional floral arabesques, painted in bright, gem-like pigments, akin to the inlaid ornamentation in semi-precious stones (*parchinkari*; *pietra-dura*), on thinly coloured or buff ground are characteristic of Shah Jahan's atelier. The illumination work in the paintings of Shah Jahan's time proclaims its affiliation with the surface ornamentation with the brilliant-coloured stones in the buildings of his reign. The borders painted during Shah Jahan's period are characterized by geometrical patterns of quatre-foils and rosettes with floral and leaf sprays, and scrolling gold palmettes and floral forms executed in bright colours. A very common decorative motif is the meander in which curves are filled with floral designs. Colours are applied in it in imitation of enamelling on gold and silver. Another favourite subject of margin-painting was full colour portraits in the borders sur-rounding the central portrait.

It seems that the one-page miniatures preserved in Mughal albums were sometimes remargined and border decoration was added to them after sometime. We find that margin decoration is not necessarily always contemporaneous to the picture in the centre of the folio. For example, the border with a spiralling arabesque of vines and blossoms added to the paint-ing 'zebra' by Mansur in 1621 (Minto Album VA, IM, no. 23-1925) is characteristic of Shah Jahan's reign. Other examples are 'Jahangir embracing Shah Abbas', c. 1618 (FGA, 45.9), and 'Jahangir preferring a sufi to kings', c. 1615–18 (FGA, 42.15), painted by Abu'l Hasan and Bichitr, respectively. Their marginpaint-ing belong to the mid-eighteenth century and were executed by Muhammad Sadiq in AH 1161/AD 1746–7. Special mention may be made of the panels of calligraphy signed by Mir 'Ali of Herat (d.1518) included in the Mughal albums. These were provided with wide illustrated margins during the seventeenth century (see Figure 12), numerous examples of which are known in the Freer Gallery of Art, Washington, D.C.; Metropolitan Museum of Art, New York; Victoria and Albert Museum, London; and Naprstek Museum, Prague.

Margin decoration had a significant place in the Mughal atelier. Abu'l Fazl has mentioned that besides the painters, illuminators, gilders, line-drawers (*jadwal-arayan*), and book-binders (*sahhaf*), too, were employed in the atelier. This suggests that illumination work was treated as a specialized branch and individuals skilled in this work were entrusted with it. We find a group of two or three illuminators decorating the borders of a particular manuscript and this is confirmed by the fact that we come across the same set of border decoration being repeated on numerous folios of the same manuscript. Generally, the margin paintings are unascribed. Though ascribed margins are few, they are important as these tell us that the artists, too, sometimes executed margin paintings and illuminated the title page (*sar-i lauh*). The margin paintings executed by Balchand, Husaini, Ikhlas, Khem, and Shivdas are

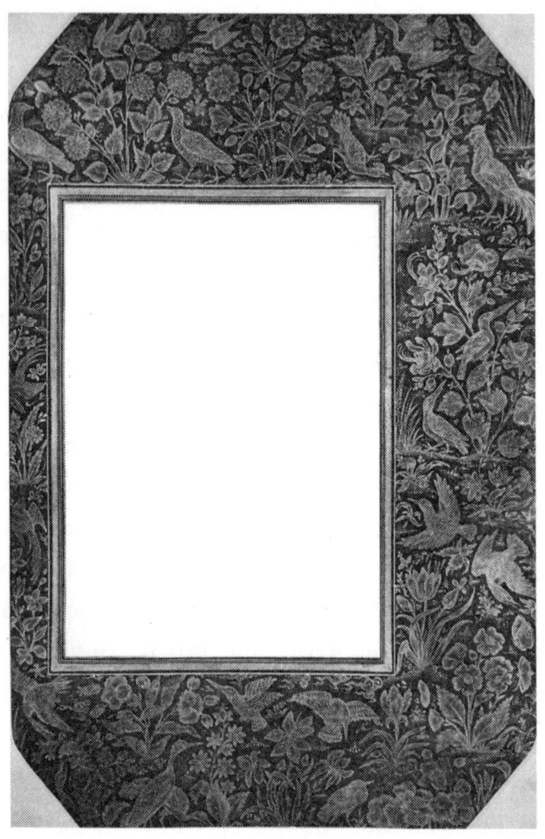

FIGURE 12 Margin decoration derived from a decorated
panel of calligraphy by Mir Ali of Herat. Bequeathed by
Lady Wantage. Victoria and Albert Museum, London
(IM, 112-A-1921).

known in the *Baharistan* of Jami, dated 1595 (BLO, Elliot MS. 254). Mansur, too, illuminated the sar-i lauh (illuminated heading) of the *Khamsa* of Amir Khusrau, dated 1597–8 (WAM W.624), the *Akbarnama* (BM, Or. 12208), dated 1604, and an undated opening page of a *Diwan* of Anwari. Aqa Riza, Bishandas, Daulat, and Govardhan are other painters known to have executed sumptuous wide borders. It is scarcely necessary to add that with the involvement of the master painters in the work of margin decoration, margin painting reached its zenith during the seventeenth century. The faithful depiction of birds and animals, and actual human portraits, and the naturalistic studies of flowering plants have no parallel in the art of Safavid Iran and pre-Muhammadan art of India.

6

Humanism in Mughal Painting

The Mughal school is not essentially the heritage of India's past. Its rise with innovations and novelties is distinct in the history of world art. Mughal patrons were not orthodox. They experimented with newer forms and techniques and assimilated them in their art. This new art is, of course, eclectic in character. The greater part of Mughal paintings belongs to the period of Akbar, Jahangir, and Shah Jahan, which reveals its proximity and contrariety with Indian, Persian, and European art. The growth of the Mughal art was fast and soon it showed contrasts with Indian and Persian traditions. In this context it is relevant to mention that the Mughal painting equipped with the tenets of European art must have fascinated contemporary observers during medieval times. Akbar's own innovative interest in social and religious communities gave rise to imagery in Indian art. Akbar and his painters opted for novel forms and techniques under the profound impact of the biblical pictures of the Renaissance period. During Jahangir's time, the use of Christian imagery became even more marked than in Akbar's time. In fact, pictures on biblical themes full of exoticisms and great naturalism inspired both the patrons and the painters.

The impact of European Renaissance art on the Mughal school became so pervasive that Mughal painting has been described as a 'hybrid blend' of the East and West. It is true that with the increasing influence of Renaissance art, the growth of both Indian and Persian elements lost their dominance in Mughal style and, so, the Mughal school cannot be described adequately without a knowledge of Renaissance art.

The Mughal school in general is heavily indebted to Renaissance art, which flourished initially in Italy during the fifteenth century. The visual realism, scientific accuracy, and careful modelling of light and shadow in the work of the Mughal school much against the concept of overall brightness in Oriental art, testifies to this fact. An emphasis on naturalism, which held a prominent place in Renaissance art (High Renaissance style, 1500–26), conditioned Mughal art.

The term 'humanism' has been associated with the Renaissance, a movement that chiefly happened in Italy during the late fourteenth to the early sixteenth centuries, and to the literary and cultural work of the great figures of the Renaissance. Humanism came to reflect itself in the arts of the Renaissance in various ways. Notably, it gave rise to a new theory of art and its techniques, especially in the use of chiaroscuro, the sense of volume, and the illusion of the three dimensions through perspective.

The Renaissance artists' notion of space viewed in linear perspective comprising seemingly three-dimensional human figures, and the like, gave rise to the search for mathematical and scientifically accurate methods of creating illusions of reality on a two-dimensional plane. This specific aim, combined with the moral and emotional aspects of painting, defined an artist's status as a practitioner of an intellectual discipline. A Renaissance artist was no more a craftsman or an imitative worker. The newly discovered principles of a vanishing-point perspective fully emphasized an accurate representation of buildings and other objects. The presentation of a diagonal view and foreshortening of proportions involved a greater sense of mathematics. The proposed system of perspective in painting thus brought together the knowledge of mathematics and art.

The humanists' interest in man gave rise to the development of portraiture where portraits with a landscape setting in the background presented an innovative form of landscape painting. In such examples, nature appears complementary to the human form. Under the impress of 'humanism', portraiture aimed at revealing unseen mysteries of the soul. 'Realism' was further reflected in Renaissance art by a new sense of mass and volume, and chiaroscuro—that is, the management of light and shade.

The Italian humanism of the late fourteenth to sixteenth centuries greatly inspired the Renaissance art of Europe on which the Mughal school so greatly drew. The visual realism, scientific accuracy, and careful modelling of light and shade, much against the concept of over-all brightness in Oriental art, seen in the Mughal school all attest to it. An emphasis on naturalism, which held a prominent place in Renaissance art, is reflected in Mughal art, the affinity being mostly with the high Renaissance style (1500–27). What is of particular interest is that the influence of Renaissance art begins to be seen in Mughal art already by the 1570s. The most notable aspect of the miniatures of the *Tutinama* (one of the earliest illustrated manuscripts from the Mughal school, datable to 1570–5, CMA) is the lively effect achieved in the depiction of figures with emphasis placed on establishing psychological relationship between them. As a result, the figures appear highly animated. Undoubtedly, these express a naturalistic and expressive quality of art which was a major feature of the developed Mughal style. An application of deep shading in the modelling of the figures and landscape shows an improvement on the strictly two-dimensional pictures of the Persian and western India schools of painting. The technique of shading employed to create a three-dimensional effect and physical tangibility seen in Basawan's work was not known to the Persian and Indian artists of the time. It is interpreted as a straightforward adaptation of methods introduced through an access to European Renaissance painting (c. 1350–1550). Still, here only a rudimentary knowledge of humanistic painting is observable, such as the technique of shading to represent mass and volume. An advance towards a better appreciation of perspective is made in the *Hamzanama* paintings (Mughal school, c. 1556–80), which sometimes exhibit human figures in the background as comparatively diminutive in size beside those in the foreground. Similarly, distant buildings shown on a diminished scale, too, emphasize depth in the painting. Two important elements in Renaissance art, modelling and perspective, had thus begun to find a place in Mughal art by 1580.

Mughal painters obviously derived their knowledge of humanism and Renaissance art from European pictures, engravings, and specimens of decorative art and textiles, which were perhaps obtained by the early 1570s. Akbar had contact with the Europeans at least since 1573.

Abu'l Fazl notices the visit of Pietro Tavares to Akbar's court at Fatehpur Sikri in 1578. Father Francis Julian Pereira, invited by Akbar to his court in 1578, was present at Fatehpur Sikri when the first Jesuit mission led by Rudolph Aquaviva and Monserrate from Goa arrived in February 1580. Most probably Akbar had acquired some specimens of European art much before 1580. European pictures of Christ, Mary, Moses, and Muhammad were already present in the royal dining-hall when the Jesuit mission arrived.

During this period, Goa itself was a thriving centre of Christian art comprising especially devotional themes. Besides the Indian artists, European artists too were active in Goa. They include the Flemish Jesuit sculptor Father Markus Mach (known as Marcos Rodirguez, d. 1601) and the Portuguese Jesuit painter Manuel Godinho (active during 1580s). The latter specialized in reproducing images of Virgin Mary. The Christian pictures still extant in the 'Maryam palace' at Fatehpur Sikri are the earliest evidence of an Indian artist's work in the Italian Renaissance style. Some such pictures are described as representing the 'Annunciation' and the 'Fall'.

The first Jesuit mission on its arrival presented a copy of Plantyn's *Royal Polyglot Bible* (printed at Antwerp between 1568 and 1573) to Akbar in 1580. Its eight volumes, sumptuously bound and clasped with gold, were illustrated with several pictures engraved by Flemish artists of the school of Quintin Matsys (1466–1530), including the work of P. Huys. These remained in the imperial library till 1595, when these were returned to the third Jesuit mission. These presumably served as one of the sources of Christian art of the Renaissance period at the Mughal atelier. The traces of the work of other Flemish artists, for example, Theodar Galle (1571–1633), Hieronymus Wierix, Johann Sadeler (1550–1600), and Raphael Sadeler (1555–1618), are found in paintings in the royal albums of the Mughal school. Undoubtedly, the large number of small engravings introduced from Europe during the late sixteenth and the beginning of the seventeenth centuries contributed much to the absorption of Renaissance humanism by Mughal art in both technique and spirit.

European pictures brought to India were in the form of illustrations in printed books, woodcuts, copper engravings, coloured pictures, and prints of European specimens published by Plantyn's firm at Antwerp. Besides, European tapestries both silken and woollen depicting stories from the Old Testament were also brought to the Mughal court. The display of Christian paintings on sacred subjects in the Jesuit chapels and churches, open to the public in general, must have enabled many artists to get more familiarized with the art of the Renaissance period. The display of European pictures on Biblical themes held at Fatehpur Sikri in 1580 was followed by one at Agra in 1602, and at Cambay during Jahangir's reign.

A large number of European pictures and engravings were gifted to the emperor, princes, and nobles by the Jesuits. In 1598, Xavier presented pictures of Christ and St Ignatius Loyola to Akbar. Again in 1601, Xavier and Pinheiro presented a picture of the Virgin drawn in ink to Akbar. The uncoloured picture apparently did not impress the emperor, for the Fathers soon presented him another picture. European portraits too were in demand, and in 1602 the Jesuits at the Mughal court presented two historical portraits, one of Albuquerque and the other of the then Portuguese Viceroy of India, Ayres de Saldagna, to Akbar.

Jahangir, even when he was a prince, showed considerable interest in Christian pictures and tried to acquire them. He often showed off his collection of Christian pictures. In 1608, Xavier noticed that Jahangir's collection included the pictures of Sardanapalus, the Circumcision, God the Father, Crucifixion, and David kneeling before Nathan. He had his audience and private assembly halls at Agra decorated with such pictures.

Though little is known about Shah Jahan's interest in European pictures, the surviving pictures from his atelier clearly evince the continuing adaptation and incorporation of European art. Nevertheless, this feature seems largely confined to the incorporation of landscape motifs and European symbols and figures. Shah Jahan's interest in the picture of Diana is attested by his reported purchase of a painting on this subject while he was a prince. But copies of European engravings (prints) and pictures were not made on the kind of scale witnessed during Jahangir's period. This would possibly suggest that Shah Jahan's interest in European art did not last long. Aurangzeb forbade the art at the court and showed no interest in paintings, Indian or European.

There was considerable demand for European pictures among nobles. In 1616, Roe presented Muqarrab Khan '13 pictures of Christ and a set of 12 of the Apostles'. In the same year, he presented to Jamaluddin Hasan Inju a book containing 48 sheets of pictures, illustrating the whole life of Christ. Mirza Beg and Asaf Khan were other nobles to whom Roe presented pictures. Aziz Koka, foster-brother of Akbar, also showed interest in Christian pictures and tried to acquire the picture of Madonna del Popolo from the Jesuits. Mahabat Khan and Zulfikhar Khan, too, had Christian pictures in their possession.

The European pictures and engravings available to the Mughal patrons and the painters largely transformed their views towards painting and aesthetic attributes. The Mughal artists, under the influence of the Renaissance humanist movement in art, added a new chapter in Indian art which is neither a direct continuation of the pre-Islamic Indian traditions nor explicitly Persian. The Mughal painting, eclectic in character, evolved with the interaction of various traditions, predominantly Indian, Persian, and European. The context of naturalism, scientific perspective, and chiaroscuro in Mughal painting is the gift of humanism as practised by the European artists of Renaissance. The Mughal artists assimilated and absorbed the new methods and techniques which characterized Renaissance art of the fifteenth and sixteenth centuries in Italy and other countries of Europe. The linear art of Persia alone did not fascinate the Mughal connoisseurs and painters. Akbar's urge for realism in art is quite clear when he sat for his painters to obtain a true and lively portrait.

A portrait in the humanistic sense is definable as a faithful portrayal of the character of an individual. An artist was now expected to work by looking at the subject and not from imagination. The Mughal paintings exhibiting artists at work bear an evidence of human portrait being drawn from life/model. Thus, fine naturalistic drawings were produced with the combined effect of light and shade and perspective. These obviously differed from the archetypes of the past. The Mughal artist's goal appears to be the portrayal of objective reality and the presentation of nature with minute and almost photographic fidelity—the very tenets of Renaissance art. Basawan, among Akbar's painters, perhaps succeeded most in the sphere and well deserves Abu'l Fazl's praise of him as a master painter with excellence in various branches of painting, including 'the drawing of features' (portraits). This technique of Renaissance art found its fuller expression during the seventeenth century, especially in the works of Bichitr, Daulat, Govardhan, and Payag.

As in Renaissance art, a kind of idealization in human portraiture also took place in the Mughal school. This included the mode of presenting the figure in isolation amidst a vast landscape; or perceptibly larger than the surroundings and thus dominating the whole landscape; or against the background of a vast open sky filled with billowing clouds. In the allegorical picture 'Jahangir embracing Shah Abbas' (FGA, no. 45.9), Abu'l Hasan presents a symbolic depiction of the Mughal emperor's power and superiority over the Shah of Iran, who is represented as the lesser partner with the figure of Jahangir shown majestically towering above him. The magnification of the favoured subject to emphasize his special secular status, or to attach divinity, has long been a tradition in Indian sculpture and painting. In another instance, in an allegorical portrait of Asaf Khan (c. 1625–30, Minto Album, VA, IM, 27-1925), executed by Bichitr, the figure of the main character dominates the whole composition and it looms large over a vast city containing clusters of buildings, high minarets, and bands of cavalry—all shown on a drastically diminished scale, suggestive of aerial perspective (see Figure 13).

Bichitr's famous portrait of Shah Jahan (c. 1635, Album, CBL, no. 16) in Chester Beatty Library, Dublin, excels both in its idealization and in the use of symbols. In this portrait, the figure of Shah Jahan is prominently depicted with a large radiating halo, standing on a

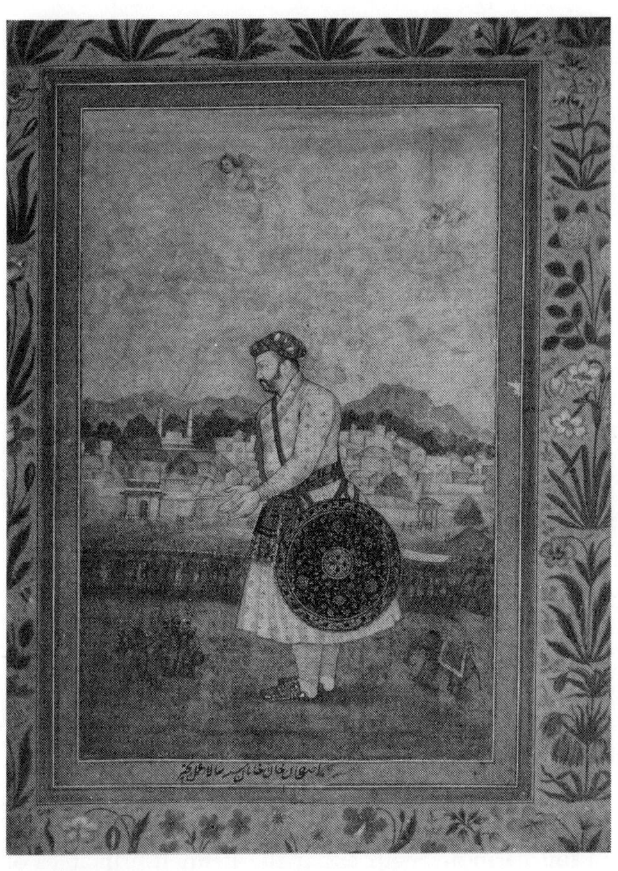

FIGURE 13 Asaf Khan. By Bichitr, c. 1640.
Minto Album, Victoria and Albert Museum, London
(IM, 27–1925).

terrestrial globe with the conventional symbol of 'lion and sheep' and the two angels descending amidst billowing clouds and holding the royal insignia (a European crown). Here, the symbolism comes right out of the conventions of European painting, practically unaltered. It certainly enriches the visual vocabulary of symbols in Mughal iconography.

In another portrait of Shah Jahan (c. 1635–7, Album, CBL), also at the Chester Beatty Library, ascribed to Payag, he is drawn standing on a terrestrial globe holding a matchlock. The background comprises horsemen storming a fort and a group of men presenting themselves before the emperor, all depicted on a drastically reduced scale and blurred in effect. The artist's understanding of the aerial perspective here is in accordance with Renaissance art. By now, the mode of drawing the main character much larger than other objects seems to have become the mainstay of the Mughal artists in the presentation of royal or aristocratic portraits.

Mughal portraits are distinct since these are not in full harmony with either the defined principles of Islamic aesthetics, or ancient and medieval Indian art. Undoubtedly, Mughal artists achieved great success in executing truly lifelike images of their subjects by

completely absorbing elements of Renaissance humanism in their art. Indeed, a few masters of the Mughal
school, namely Basawan, Bichitr, Daulat, Govardhan,
Mirar (or Murar), and Payag, could even reach the acu-
men of the great Renaissance artists.

Mention may be made here of Kesavdas, a painter of
Akbar's court and best known for copies of European
works. His picture 'St Matthew and the angel' (BLO),
executed in 1587–8, was based on a print of an engraving by Philip Galle after Maarten van Heemskrek's
'St Matthew the Evangelist' and is almost European in
character. In his copy, the Mughal painter has successfully delineated the folds in the robes of the saint and
the facial expression in his figure. Kesavdas's painting
'Joseph telling his dream to his father' (c. 1580–5, CBL),
based on an engraving by George Pencz, dated 1544,
is another outstanding Mughal copy of a European
work, revealing the artist's full control over European
technique and style. In his picture of St Jerome,
adapted from Mario Cartaro's print of an engraving of
Michelangelo's Noah from Sistine Chapel, Kesavdas's
understanding of the subject is explicit in the rendering of the muscular modelling close to the style of
Michelangelo. In fact, Kesavdas has excelled here. The

pulsating flesh of his image is more Michelangelesque than the Italian engraving he copied. We know that almost identical Mughal versions of European engravings or pictures were not uncommon in Mughal India. Abu'l Hasan, with equal mastery, adapted his technique to the trends and modes of Renaissance art. His picture 'St John' (Ashmolean Museum, Oxford), executed in monochrome at the age of 13 in 1601, after an engraving by Durer, clearly reveals his deep understanding of three-dimensional representations. Another picture of his, 'Roman sea-god Neptune riding on a water horse' (BKB), the European source of which is not clear, is fully expressive of the tenets of Renaissance art. The number of Mughal pictures showing a straightforward imitation of European themes and adaptation of their techniques and methods is quite large (see Figure 14). In general, these exhibit great understanding of the chiaroscuro technique, modelling of physical features, and visual effects in the treatment of space. Deep shading, controlled light effect, and heavy modelling were employed in the Mughal style to project volume as well. The Mughal painters somewhat understood the principles of light and shade and used spotlight-effect and cast-shadows in their work. The

Oriental method was to depict objects fully bathed in light and to treat day and night scenes in the same fashion, with the difference of the introduction of a candle in the foreground, or a starlit sky with moon to convey the impression that the event was taking place in darkness. On the other hand, some of the seventeenth-century miniatures like 'Ascetics seated round a fire' or 'A prince visiting an ascetic during the night' or 'An assembly of learned men during the night' show glowing faces of individuals, and the rest of the scene finished in dark pigment; no symbols are needed to tell us that we have a night scene here.

The European perspective largely influenced the Mughal visual perception and the methods of handling space in painting. However, the Mughal painter never fully understood it, and therefore, the convergence of angels and diagonal views of buildings do not appear with the same felicity as in European art. A gradual receding effect in landscape was not always well achieved in their work. Mughal artists failed to grasp the mathematical and scientifically accurate methods of creating illusions of reality on a two-dimensional plane. One must here realize that the adoption of Renaissance humanism in Mughal art was not the

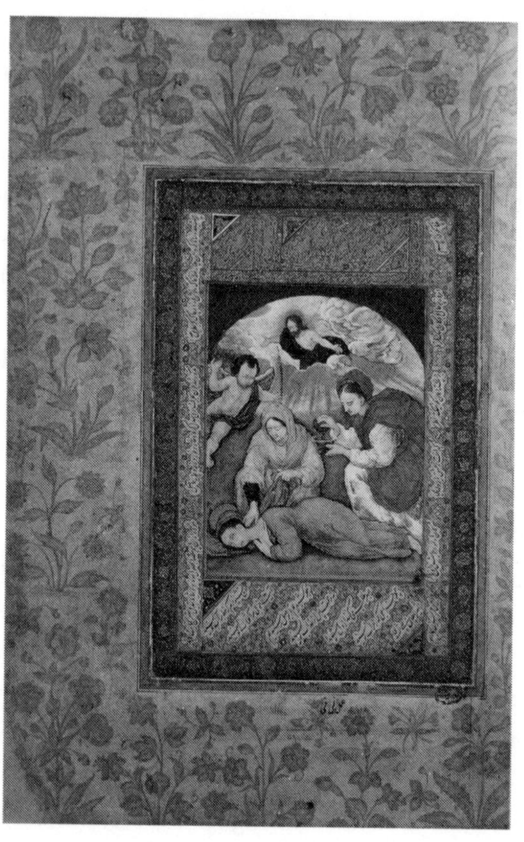

FIGURE 14 The Martyrdom of Saint Cecilia. By Nini;
after an engraving by Jerome [Hieronymus] Wierix, c. 1600.
Bequeathed by Lady Wantage. Victoria and Albert Museum,
London (IM, 139–1921).

result of an intellectual or scientific movement, and this certainly handicapped it in appreciating the full import of Europe's achievement in art.

Mughal painters could not, after all, liberate themselves from the canons of the conventional arts of Persia and India, though their conscious effort to switch over to the methods and techniques of Renaissance art showed both skill and ingenuity.

The modes and trends of Renaissance art of Europe, with their humanist message, gained popularity in the Mughal school, but faded away soon afterwards since other contemporary or near contemporary schools of Indian art hardly got influenced by them. The 'realism' of Renaissance art has no place in the classical Indian art and the tenets of high Mughal style (first quarter of the seventeenth century), heavily burdened with the concept of physical reality, are not in harmony with the trends of classical Indian art. Havell has rightly remarked:

> The academic tradition of Hindu and Buddhist sculpture and painting was, and is still, entirely based upon symbolism, and without the knowledge for interpreting it no one can enter deeply into the study of any branch of Indian art.... The gulf which divides East

and West is that which separates realism from idealism.... India insists that what we call reality is deceptive and untruthful, and strives to express it through the ideal.

However, during the late nineteenth century, with the awakening among the Indian intelligentsia, especially in Bengal, there emerged a change in the ideas about art and aesthetics. With the rise of nationalism there emerged a renewed interest and pride in the culture heritage. Raja Ravi Varma's (b. 1848) paintings, which are representative of Western academic manner and imbibe tenets of the Renaissance art of Europe, turned out to be a strong channel of transference of Western realism into Indian art. In response to the emerging nationalism, Varma turned to themes from Indian mythology and history, but always adhered to Western technique and style of painting. His narratives and portraits are best known for chiaroscuro effect of light and shade, heavy modelling, and deep shading—all complementary to the naturalism in art. His human figures are idealized to show the physical charm of the human body. Indian art witnessed another change at the end of the nineteenth century;

with the rise of the new 'Indian style', heralded by Abanindranath Tagore and followed by Asit Kumar Haldar, Surendra Nath Ganguly, Nandlal Bose, Abdur Rahman Chughtai, and others, there developed the Bengal school of painting (also called the Nationalist school), which totally discarded Western academic art. The basic difference between the two forms was in their approach to art. The bases of European art were purely scientific and mathematical concepts, encompassing 'modernization', while in the case of Indian art the main thrust was to glorify the past and to insist on a total denial of Western art concepts. Thus, the chapter of 'humanism' in art that entered Indian art with the Mughal school diminished with the rise of the Nationalist school.

7

Artists' Signatures

The identification of paintings as works of particular artists is always one of the major preoccupations of the students of art history. The first basis of such identification has been the artist's signature, which is practically universal in Western art since the Renaissance. In India, writings describing the themes of paintings and giving the names of the artists first appear with the Mughal school in the sixteenth and seventeenth centuries.

The Mughal school of painting originated under Akbar, at whose court a large number of illuminated manuscripts were prepared; and these contain the bulk of the miniatures that survive from his reign. Here, as the scribe wrote the text, large blank spaces were left for miniatures, which were painted later, largely to suit the text at the point where the illustrations were put in.

Sometimes artists were also given specific instructions in writing at the bottom of the blank spaces about what to depict. Numerous such inscriptions have survived on the illustrations, though many of them were later wholly or partly covered under the pigments laid on them by the painter, or by the placement of the marginal lines and illumination work. Similarly, album pictures, especially portraits, often bore short inscriptions indicating the persons portrayed. Besides these inscriptions concerned with themes, the most common are those which simply give the names of the painters.

The historicity of many Mughal miniatures thus depends on the inscriptions they contain and such miniatures in their turn become a point of reference for the characteristics of style and technique helping to establish the date, provenance, and even the authorship of unascribed paintings.

Although our understanding of the Mughal school depends on these short texts found in Mughal miniatures, their study has been surprisingly neglected. Many catalogues of well-known collections do not even list the texts of the inscriptions and often enough omit translations. Even when the paintings are reproduced in print, the inscriptions are sometimes left out, or so dimly printed as to be illegible, and there is almost no attempt to reproduce the inscriptions separately on an enlarged scale. The decipherments or readings also occasionally leave much to be desired. Except for some attention paid to imperial autographs, there has been almost no discussion of the styles of writings or individual hands appearing in these inscriptions. It is this general neglect that has apparently led to a surprising lapse on the part of almost all students of Mughal miniatures.

There is the lack of all distinction between two important kinds of inscriptions: (*a*) the artist's own signatures, or inscriptions written by the artist; and (*b*) 'third-person ascriptions', that is, inscriptions written by the scribe or the patron (including the emperor) or some other person, ascribing the painting to an artist or artists (in case of a joint work). Overlooking later forgeries, though both the categories are of importance for identifying works of individual artists, the first is of still greater significance since it tells us more about the artist.

In spite of the obvious importance of the artists' signatures for the historians of Mughal art, cataloguers uniformly tend to mix up third-person ascriptions with actual signatures. Thus, Stchoukine (1929b) in his otherwise careful catalogue of the paintings lodged in the Musee du Louvre has referred to 'third-person ascriptions' as 'signatures'. Gray (1948) and Welch (1963) in their exhibition catalogues have described such ascribed miniatures as signed works. Martin (1912) has mentioned some of the paintings executed by Hashim, Hunhar, Anupchhatr, and others as 'signed works', presumably taking the ascriptions to be signatures. The present study will show that the works of these painters do not belong to the category of 'signed works'.

The 'third-person ascriptions' can easily be identified as such, since in accordance with the Persian usage of the time, these contain no suggestion of humility or self-abasement to the names given. Thus, the phrase *'amal-i Daswant* (work of Daswant) is a third-person ascription; so also is *tarh-i Daswant*, *'amal-i Miskin* (sketch by Daswant, colouring by Miskin). These ascriptions generally tend to be in the scribes' standard *nasta'liq* and not in an informal or ordinary hand. This too rules out their being 'signatures'.

This practice of recording the names of the artists on their works seems to have been followed by the

Mughal school after the trend in the fifteenth-century art of Persia (Safavid and Timurid art). However, the earliest illustrations of the Mughal school, namely the *Hamzanama* (c. 1565–70), the *Anwar-i Suhaili* (SOAS, dated 1570), and so on, are invariably unascribed. The earliest ascribed paintings are the works of Mir Sayyid ʿAli and Khwaja ʿAbdu-s Samad, but the latter already gives us his signatures on some of his works.

In general, the practice of the artist's name being recorded on the miniatures seems to have become common after 1580. Such examples are the illustrations of the manuscripts *Razmnama* (c. 1580–4), *Taʾrikh-i Khandan-i Timuria* (c. 1584–6), and the *Diwan-i Hafiz* (c. 1585). Here the ascriptions appear below, on the margins, written in one or two hands, evidently by the scribe of the atelier. In such third-person ascriptions, the artists' names are preceded by the word *ʿamal* or *kar* or *mashq*. So, where the miniature is the work of a single artist, we have *ʿamal-i Basawan* (work of Basawan), and so forth. In joint works, terms like *tarh* (sketching), *rangamezi* (colouring), and *ʿamal* (work in general, or specifically colouring) are employed, for example, *tarh-i Basawan*, *ʿamal-i Bhura* (sketch by Basawan, colouring by Bhura). When a third painter also collaborated and finished the portraits, figures, and the like, he is credited with *chihra* or *chihranami* and *surat*, for example, *tarh-i Basawan*, '*amal-i Nand Gawalyari, chihra Madhav*. The method continued into the seventeenth century, though by then manuscript painting had undergone a decline, the emphasis being shifted to portrait painting. It is, however, intriguing that a good number of illustrations are left unascribed. The same is true of album pictures. The reason for this omission is difficult to discover and speculations on this at present are not likely to be very fruitful.

A scrutiny of the inscriptions on the miniatures during the sixteenth century suggests that there was almost no scope for the artists' own signatures in manuscript paintings; ascriptions were written by the scribe or the 'record-keeper' of the *taswirkhana*. On the other hand, album pictures tended to bear the artists' signatures. The album pictures also contain 'third-person ascriptions' in a scribe's hand and, on a few rare occasions, by the royal patron himself.

As for the artists' signatures proper, these can be identified by the well-known Persian (and Indo-Persian) usage whereby a person writing his name in his own hand invariably used a word or phrase in self-abasement, which no one would use for a third person. Thus, on documents and seals we have words like *'al-'abd* (slave), *fidwi* (devoted servant), *faqir* (indigent), *banda* (slave), and so on, preceding or following the name. When we examine the inscriptions on the miniatures, the signed inscriptions immediately strike us, for they contain phrases like *'al-'abd, banda-i ikhlas* (sincere slave), *banda-i dargah* (slave of the court), *banda-i Padshah* (slave of the king), *banda-i kamtarin* (the humblest slave), *faqir* (indigent), *faqir-ul haqir* (the humblest indigent person), *ghulam ba ikhlas* (sincere slave), *murid ba ikhlas* (sincere disciple), *banda-i dargah kamtarin* (the humblest slave of the court), *kamtarin* (the humblest slave), *kamtarin muridzada* (the humblest son of a disciple), *banda-i shikasta raqam* (unskilled slave), and so on.

Given this simple but (in Persian usage) well-established criterion, we can go on to identify the signatures of individual artists. In the process of compiling a comprehensive catalogue of Mughal artists' works, I have studied practically all the catalogued items and personally inspected a very large number of miniatures in various collections. The following survey of artists' signatures is based on this work. Painters at Akbar's atelier usually did not put their signatures on their creations; Khwaja 'Abdu-s Samad and Kesavdas form the sole exceptions. Aqa Riza, a painter from Salim's studio, contemporary to the painters mentioned above, too signed some of his miniatures. No signed miniature is known from 'Abdur Rahim Khan-i Khanan's library where we only have 'third-person ascriptions'.

In Jahangir's reign, signed paintings become distinctly more numerous. Notable amongst the painters who signed their miniatures in the seventeenth century are Abu'l Hasan, Balchand, Bichitr, Daulat, Govardhan, Manohar, Mansur, and Mirar (Murar or Murad). The practice of signing miniatures thus grew with time, although some master painters of the reigns of Jahangir and Shah Jahan such as Bishandas, Hashim, Hunhar, Muhammad Nadir, Chitarman, and Anupchhatr are still known to us through 'third-person ascriptions' only.

All the signatures we have are in the Persian language, and this suggests that several Hindu painters such as Balchand, Bichitr, Govardhan, Manohar, and Payag must have acquired a knowledge of Persian. There is just one exception: Kesavdas, who in 1588–9 signed his work in Devanagari.

Inscriptions intended to be signatures mostly appear on the picture itself; some of the artists' signatures are affixed on the margins outside the picture frame as well. In some cases signatures are partly hidden, being put on unimportant objects shown in the paintings, for example, on a utensil, footstool, book, architectural column, rock, and the like. Aqa Riza, Daulat, and Mansur are usually fond of this eccentricity and they sometimes give dates as well.

While a distinction between the 'third-person ascriptions' and signatures introduces a new element in the work of identifying Mughal miniatures, a closer study of the text and writing itself is recommended for distinguishing forgeries from genuine works. Thus, when we have recognized certain signatures of artists as such, we can familiarize ourselves with the specific feature of their handwriting. Once we do so, we can be in a better position to detect forged signatures. Thus, we find that the famous artist Bichitr in his signatures always writes his name as Bichitr. Yet, in a very striking painting of 'A prince on the back of an elephant' (IM), we get following signature: *'Amal-i ghulam ba-ikhlas Bichhitr, 1016* (Work of the loyal slave, Bichhitr, AD 1607–8). Clearly, this has been forged by someone who overlooked the fact that Bichitr never inducted *ha* (to become *chh*) into the spelling of his name. The fact of forgery is reinforced by the text of the preceding inscription: *Shahzada Muhammad Murad farzind-i Shah Jahan bar fil Iqbal* (Prince Muhammad Murad, son of Shah Jahan, on the elephant Iqbal). The name of Prince Murad was Murad Bakhsh and not Muhammad Murad. This was a mistake Bichitr, being at the court, could never have made. Moreover, in AH 1016 (AD 1607–8), the year given in the signature, Prince Murad was not even born. Thus, the fact of forgery, suggested by the style of writing, is proved beyond dispute by the actual contents of the inscription.

In conclusion, one would recommend certain basic minimum rules to be followed in all future cataloguing of Mughal miniatures. The text of all inscriptions on the miniatures must be given in full in the original (with or without translation), and there should be a description of the hand in which it is written, for example, formal or scribe's *naskh* or nasta'liq; rapid hand or nasta'liq; *shikasta-amez* or ordinary with abbreviated form; and *shikasta* or shorthand. Wherever possible, the texts of signatures (as distinct from 'third-person ascriptions') should be reproduced in a size large enough to be legible, with the scale of the original being indicated. Where this is not possible, the cataloguer may mention whether the hand in a signature is similar or not to the hand found in other signatures of the same artist. We would then be in a much stronger position to judge the genuineness of all 'signed' miniatures.

Conclusion

Mughal painting, unique in style and thematically varied, initially attracted connoisseurs and critics of art for its aesthetic attributes. Nevertheless, its great importance lies in its being a 'socio-cultural phenomenon' in the history of Indian art. The subjective approach of the artist establishes his commitment to the worldly life. He was intimately involved with the physical reality of his subject, which drew him close to his surroundings. In brief, Mughal painting as a document is a reflection of the life of the times.

The development of various branches of art at the Mughal studio, that is, self-portraiture, historical portraits, paintings with zoological themes, and margin-painting that reached its zenith at the Mughal atelier, while adding new chapters to Indian art history, also opened new vistas to painting for future generations. The manuscript painting and illuminating work attained great perfection and became a more living and active tradition than in the past. Illustrated manuscripts on themes other than the religious emerged and opened the way to a fresh conceptual and stylistic expression of art. The Mughal narratives do not evoke religious sentiment and it makes the Mughal school decidedly secular. With the Mughal school the spiritual and transcendental were not the leitmotif.

The Mughal artist's realistic approach to his subject is a marked departure from the mannered style of the art of Persia. Also, he was never attracted to the stylized human form with certain symbolic features in accordance with iconographic traditions. In fact, an advance of the Mughal artists towards a better appreciation of Renaissance humanism proved to be a strong channel of transference of European realism to Indian art. Under the influence of the Renaissance humanist movement, Mughal artists added a new chapter in art which is neither a direct continuation of the pre-Islamic Indian traditions and nor explicitly Persian. Jahangir's humanistic vision in art finally led to a change in Mughal taste and aesthetics which brushed aside the past and present of Persian and Indian paintings. The linear art of Persia and an idealized form of Indian art did not fascinate the Mughal patrons and painters and their urge for visual realism attained its solace in the Renaissance art of Europe of the fifteenth and sixteenth centuries. Their admiration for and awakening to the new art concept and their devoted endeavour towards its adoption reinterpreted Islamic and Indian aesthetics, and there developed a novel art—the Mughal rational art, a rare gift to humanity. In general, Mughal miniatures are non-symbolic historical documents of contemporary life. Mughal artists preferred a naturalistic portrayal of objects. Their perception of the portrayal of physical reality and their constant craving for individuality influenced the Mughal style. Undoubtedly, the Mughal artist was a creative synthesizer, and his artistic innovations are thus a distinctive contribution to the history of world art. In fact, the uniqueness of the Mughal school lies in its ability to adapt contemporary trends in art as a device to fulfil the demands of its patrons and its painters' creative expression.

Appendix

Major Illustrated Manuscripts

Hamzanama (VMB, MMA, FGA, FAM, BKB, BM, and CSM), c. 1556–80 (still continuing). The twelve volumes had been completed well before 1595 (Abu'l Fazl (1595), I, 115).

Deval Rani Khizr Khan (NM), c. 1567. Date assigned on stylistic grounds.

Anwar-i Suhaili (SOAS), 1570. Date of Colophon.

Tutinama (CMA), c. 1570–5. Period assigned on stylistic grounds.

Diwan of Anwari (FAM), 1580. Date of Colophon.

Gulistan of Sa'di (RAS), 1581. Date of Colophon.

Diwan-i Hafiz (CBL), 1582. Date of Colophon.

Kitab-i S'aat (H. Kevorkian Collection), 1583. Colophon; Navin Kumar Collection, New York, 1584. Colophon; Album 2, RRL, c. 1585–90. Period assigned on stylistic grounds.

Razmnama (SMS), c. 1584. Daswant, who worked on various miniatures in this volume, died in 1584. Abu'l Fazl's preface, dated 1588, seems to have been added later.

Diwan-i Hafiz (RRL), c. 1585. Period assigned on stylistic grounds.

Ta'rikh-i Khandan-i Timuria (OPL), c. 1584–5. Daswant, died 1584, worked on the first illustrated miniature.

Ramayana (SMS), 1587. Date of Colophon.

Darabnama (BM), c. 1585–90. Period assigned on stylistic grounds.

Gulistan of Sa'di (BM), c. 1590. Period assigned on stylistic grounds.

Khamsa of Nizami (CK). In an early manuscript (colophon: 1506), miniatures were overpainted c. 1585–90, the period being determined on stylistic grounds.

Kathasaritsagar (CACA), c. 1590. Period assigned on stylistic grounds.

Harivansha (VA), c. 1590. Year assigned on stylistic grounds.

Akhbar-i Barmakiyan (Colnaghi, London), c. 1595. Period assigned on stylistic grounds.

Khamsa of Nizami (BM), 1596–7. Date of Colophon. But illustration on colophon–page itself painted in 1610, date given on miniature.

Anwar-i Suhaili (BKB), 1596–97. Date of Colophon.

Khamsa of Amir Khusrau (WAG), 1597–8. Date of Colophon.

Jami'ut Tawarikh (IL), 1598. Date of Colophon.

Razmnama (SMPG), 1598. Date of Colophon.

Ramayan (FGA), 1598–9. Date of Colophon.

Zafarnama (BM), 1600. Date of Colophon.

'Iyar-i Danish (CBL), c. 1590–1600. Period assigned on stylistic grounds.

A'in-i Sikandari (MMA), c. 1595–1600. Period assigned on stylistic grounds.

Ta'rikh-i Alfi (CAG), c. 1595–1600. Period assigned on stylistic grounds.

Baharistan (BLO), c. 1595–1600. Period assigned on stylistic grounds.

Baburnama (NM), 1598 (date on folio 116).

Baburnama (BM), c. 1598. The translation of *Baburnama* by 'Abdu'r Rahim Khan-i Khanan was presented to Akbar in 1598 (Abu'l Fazl [1601], III, 862), and the present manuscript, probably a copy prepared for Akbar, was prepared at that time.

Baburnama (WAG), c. 1598. Dated on stylistic grounds.

Baburnama (SMOC), c. 1598. The style is similar to that employed in *Baburnama* (NM).

Baburnama (ML), c. 1598. The style is similar to that seen in Baburnama (WAG); (SMOC).

Akhlaq-i Nasiri (Prince Sadruddin Aga Khan Collection, Geneva), c. 1600. Dated on stylistic grounds.

Shahnama of Firdausi (BLO), c. 1600. Dated on stylistic grounds.

Shahnama (CBL), c. 1600. Dated on stylistic grounds.

Laila-e Majnun (IOL). Colophon date 1557, but miniatures added later, c. 1600.

Laila-e Majnun (BLO), c. 1600 (colophon date, 1563). Miniatures were added later.

Jog-Bashisht (CBL), 1602. Date of Colophon.

Diwan of Amir Nizamuddin Hasan (WAG), 1602. Date of Colophon.

Nufhat'al'uns (BM), 1602–3. Date of Colophon.

Raj Kunwar (CBL), 1603–4. Date of Colophon.

Akbarnama (BM), 1604. Date on miniature on folio 134b.

Akbarnama (CBL), 1604. Since this constitutes Vol. II and part III of the set of which BM constitutes Vol. I, the date may be deemed about the same.

Akbarnama (VA), c. 1602–5. Period assigned on stylistic grounds.

Razmnama (BAAC), c. 1600–5. Dated on stylistic grounds.

Anwar-i Suhaili (BM), 1610–11. Date of Colophon. But miniature on folio 54 dated 1604–5.

Bostan of Sa'di (FAM), 1605. Date of Colophon.

'Aja'ib al Makhluqat (CBL), c. 1600–5. Period assigned on stylistic grounds.

Khamsa of Mir 'Ali Shir Nawai (RLWC). Colophon, 1492, but Mughal miniatures overpainted, which are dated c. 1605.

Shahnama (BM), c. 1605–10. Date assigned on stylistic grounds.

Diwan-i Hafiz (BM), c. 1610. Date assigned on stylistic grounds.

Gulistan (BM). Colophon, 1567, but miniatures added later, c. 1605–27.

Silsilah-al Dhahab (CBL), 1613. Date of Colophon.

Soz-o Gudaz (BM), c. 1630. Date determined on stylistic grounds.

Gulistan (BLO), 1646. Date of Colophon.

Kulliyat of Sa'di (CBL), 1646. Date of Colophon.

Padshahnama (RLWC). Date of Colophon, 1657. Miniatures in this went on being inserted or added, some being painted as early as Jahangir's reign, others as late as the eighteenth century.

Majma'-al Ghara-ib (CBL), c. 1650–60. Date assigned on stylistic grounds.

Masnavi of Zafar Khan (RAS), 1662. Date of Colophon.

Glossary

'al'-'abd	slave, devotee (word prefacing a signature)
Allah-o Akbar	'God is Great' (Muslim invocation)
'amal	work (especially) execution of painting, colouring
banda	slave, servant
banda-i dargah	slave of the court (person in emperor's service)
banda-i daulat	slave of the state (person in emperor's service)
banda-i ikhlas	loyal (or sincere) slave
chihra	face, portrait
chihranami, nami chihra	lit., illustrious face; portrait of emperor or prince
dam	copper coin (worth 1/40 of rupee in Akbar's time)

dargah	mausoleum of a Muslim mystic
darogha	superintendent
dhoti	cloth worn about the waist by men, drawn between the legs and fastened behind
diwan	collection of poems
faqir	needy, destitute; conventionally employed with reference to self
faqir-al haqir	humble, destitute; conventionally employed with reference to self
ghulam	slave
hashiya	border, margin
islah	correction; improvement (e.g. of pupil's work by teacher or master)
jadwal	marginal lines; set of lines; table
jadwal-arayan	line-drawers; margin ornamentors
jama	double-breasted coat tied to one side: to the right by Muslims, to the left by Hindus
kahar	palanquin-bearer
kamtarin	lowliest, most humble; conventionally employed with reference to self
kar	work
khat	line; margin; writing
khanazad	imperial house-born

kitabkhana	library
mansab	rank in the Mughal service
mashq	writing; drawing (painting)
masnavi	Islamic narrative poem
mulla	Muslim theologian or scholar
muraqqa'	album (containing miniatures and specimens of calligraphy)
murid	disciple; imperial servant
musauwir	painter; artist
naqqashkhana	'painting-house'; atelier
nasta'liq	style of Persian writing, with rounded letters
qalam	pen; style of writing or painting
rubab	stringed musical instrument, played with a plectrum
rangamezi	colouring; colour mixing
raqam	'work by pen or brush'; writing, here painting
sangtarash	stonemason
sar-i lauh	'upper side of tablet'; illuminated heading or title page
sawar	horseman; rank expressed in numerals, indicating the number of horseman to be maintained by the *mansabdar* (holder of rank)

shikasta	'broken'; cursive (short-hand) mode of Persian writing
shirin qalam	'sweet pen'; title awarded to scribe at Mughal court
simurgh	mythical bird in Persian literature in Firdausi's *Shahnama*, the foster father of Zal, Rustam's father
siyahi qalam	term used by some modern writers for the technique of finishing painting, usually in fine black shading
suba	Mughal province
surat	figure; portrait painting
tarh	sketch; outline; drawing
taswir	picture; portrait
taswirkhana	painting-house; atelier
Tauhid-i Ilahi	'Unity of God' (in modern scholarly usage after Bada'uni); Akbar's spiritual teachings (the so-called *Din-i Ilahi*)
ustad	teacher; master painter
zat	rank expressed in numerals, which indicated the holder's personal pay and status in Mughal hierarchy
zenana	women's quarters in a mansion or palace

Bibliography

'Abdu-l Baqi Nihawandi. *Ma'asir-i Rahimi* (1616). Ed. H. Hosain, Bib. Ind., Calcutta, 1910–31. Painters noticed: Bahbud (ff. 753 a, b), Madhav (f. 753b), Maulana Ibrahim *Naqqash* (f. 754b), Maulana Mushfiq (f. 753b), Miyan Nadim (f. 753a).

Abu'l Fazl. *Akbarnama* (1601). Ed. Ahmad Ali and Abdur Rahim, Bib. Ind., Calcutta, 1873–87, tr. H. Beveridge, RAS, Calcutta, 1897–1921. Painter noticed: Daswant (III, 651).

Abu'l Fazl. *Ain-i Akbari* (1595). Ed. H. Blochmann, Bib. Ind., Calcutta, 1867–77, tr. in 3 vols, vol. I by H. Blochmann (1868), vols II and III by H.S. Jarrett (1894). Revised by D.C. Phillpott (I, 1927, 1939), J. Sarkar (II and III, 1949). Painters noticed: Bihzad (I, 113), Mir Sayyid 'Ali (I, 114, 660, no. 25), Khwaja 'Abdu-s Samad (I, 114, 554, no. 266), Muhammad Sharif (I, 582, no. 351), Daswant, Basawan, Kesav, La'l, Mukund, Miskin, Farrukh Qalmaq, Madhav,

Jagan, Mahesh, Khemkaran, Tara, Sanwala, Haribans, and Ram (I, 114), Amir Beg (I, 670, no. 41).

Arnold, Sir T.W. and L. Binyon (1921). *The Court Painters of the Grand Moghuls*, Oxford.

Arnold, Sir T.W. and J.V.S. Wilkinson (1936). *The Library of A. Chester Beatty: A Catalogue of the Indian Miniatures*, 3 vols, London.

Atabai, Badri (1353) [Iranian Solar]. *Fehrist-i Muraqqat-i Kitab Khana-i Saltanati*, Tehran, Shamsi.

Babur, *Baburnama* or *Tuzuk-i Baburi* (1530), Turki text. Ed. A.S. Beveridge, Leiden and London, 1905; Persian tr. by ‘Abdu’r Rahim Khan-i Khanan (1590), BM, Or. 3714; tr. J. Leyden and W. Erskine, revised L. King, Oxford, 1921; and A.S. Beveridge, London, 1921; Thackston, M. Wheeler, ed., tr. and annotated, New York, 1996. Painters noticed: Bihzad (291); Shah Muzaffar (291).

Bad’auni, ‘Abdul Qadir, *Muntakhabu-t Tawarikh* (1595). Ed. Ahmad Ali and Lees, Bib. Ind., Calcutta, 1864–9; tr. Ranking (I, 1898), Lowe (II, 1924), Haig (III, 1925), RAS, Calcutta.

Barrett, D. and B. Gray (1963). *Painting of India*, Lausanne.

Bayazid Bayat, *Tazkira-i Humayun-o Akbar* (1585). Ed. M. Hidayat Hosain (1941), Bib. Ind., Calcutta.

Beach, M.C. (1978). *The Grand Mogul: Imperial Painting in India (1600–60)*. Williamstown, Mass.

——— (1981). *The Imperial Image: Paintings for the Mughal Court*. Washington, D.C.

Beach, M.C. (1987). *Early Mughal Painting*. Cambridge.

——————— (1992). *Mughal and Rajput Painting*. The New Cambridge History of India, vol. 1:3. Cambridge.

Beach, M.C., Ebba Koch, and W. Thackston (1997). *King of the World: The Padshahnama, an Imperial Mughal Manuscript from the Royal Library*. London.

Beach, M.C., E. Fischer, and B.N. Goswamy (eds) (2011). *Masters of Indian Painting*, 2 vols. Ascona.

Begley, E. Wayne and Z.A. Desai (1990). *The Shah Jahan Nama of Inayat Khan*. New Delhi.

Bernier, Francois (1916). *Travels in the Mughal Empire 1656–58*, tr. A. Constable, revised V.A. Smith. London.

Bhakkari, Shaikh Farid (1961). *Zakhirat-ul Khwanin*, ed. Syed Moinul Haq. Karachi.

Binyon, L. (1913), *Painting in the Far East*, second edition. London.

Brand, Michael and G.D. Lowry (1985). *Akbar's India: Art from the Mughal City of Victory*. New York.

Brown, Percy (1924). *Indian Painting under the Mughals, A.D. 1550 to A.D. 1750*. Oxford.

Bussagli, Mario (1969). *Indian Miniatures*. London.

Chandra, Moti (1946). *The Technique of Mughal Painting*, Lucknow.

Clarke, C.S. (1921). *Twelve Mughal Paintings of the School of Humayun*. London.

——————— (1922). *Victoria and Albert Museum Drawings: Thirty Mogul Paintings from the School of Jahangir (17th century) and Four Panels of Calligraphy in the Wantage Bequest.* London.

Coomaraswamy, A.K. (1930). *Catalogue of the Indian Collections in the Museum of Fine Arts, Boston, Pt. VI (Mughal Paining).* Boston.

Das, Asok K. (1978). *Mughal Painting during Jahangir's Time.* Calcutta.

——— (1982). *Dawn of Mughal Painting.* Bombay.

——— (ed.) (1998). *Mughal Masters: Further Studies.* Mumbai.

Egger, G. (1974) and (1982). *Hamzanama,* 2 vol. Graz.

Falk, Toby and Mildred Archer (1981). *Indian Miniatures in the India Office Library.* London.

Foster, W. (ed.) (1899). *The Embassy of Sir Thomas Roe to India 1615–19.* London.

Gray, Basil (1948). 'Painting'. In Leigh Ashton (ed.), *The Art of India and Pakistan: A Commemorative Catalogue of the Exhibition Held at the Royal Academy of the Arts, 1947–8.* London: Faber and Faber, pp. 85–103.

Hejek, Lubor (1960). *Indian Miniatures of the Mughal School.* London.

Havell, E.B. (1908). *Indian Sculpture and Painting.* London.

——— (1909). 'The Symbolism in Indian Sculpture and Painting', *Burlington Magazine,* London, XV (XXVIII).

——— (1964). *The Art Heritage of India.* Bombay.

Ivanova, A.A., O.F. Akimushkin, T.V. Grek, and P.L.T. Gyuzalyana (1962). *Al'bom Indiyskikh-i Pyersidskikh*

Miniatyar XVI–XVIIIvv, Moscow, Russian text with English resume.

Jahangir, *Tuzuk-i Jahangiri* (1624). Ed. S. Ahmad, Ghazipur and Aligarh, 1863–4; tr. A. Rogers, ed. H. Beveridge, London, 1904–14; Thackston, M. Wheeler, ed. and tr. *The Jahangirnama*, New York, 1999. Painters noticed: 'Abdu-s Samad (I, 15), Abu'l Hasan (II, 20); Aqa Riza (II, 20); Bishandas (II, 116–17); Farrukh Beg (I, 159); Mansur (II, 20, 108, 145, 157); Muhammad Sharif (I, 14).

Jauhar. *Tezkereh al Vakiat* (1587), tr. Stewart. *Private Memoirs of the Mughal Emperor Humayun*, 1832. London.

Khandalavala, K. (1938). *Indian Sculpture and Painting: An Introductory Study*. Bombay.

Khandalavala, K. and Moti Chandra (1965). *Miniatures and Sculptures, Collection of Sir Cowasji Jehangir*. Bombay.

Koch, Ebba (2001). *Mughal Art and Imperial Ideology: Collected Essays*. New Delhi.

Kuhnel, Ernst and H. Goetz (1926). *Indian Book Painting*. London.

Losty, J.P. (1982). *The Art of the Book in India (Catalogue of an Exhibition Mounted at the British Library from 16 April– 1 August 1982)*. London.

Maclagan, E.D. (1932). *The Jesuits and the Great Mogul*. London.

Martin, F.R. (1912). *The Miniature Painting and Painters of Persia, India and Turkey*. London.

Mehta, N.C. (1926). *Studies in Indian Painting*. Bombay.

Minorsky, T., (tr.) (1959). *Calligraphers and Painters: A Treatise by Qazi Ahmad Son of Mir Munshi, circa AH 1015 (AD 1606)*. Washington.

Monserrate, S.J. (1922). *The Commentary of Father Monserrate, S.J. on his journey to the court of Akbar*, tr. J.S. Hoyland, annotated by S.N. Banerjee. London.

Muqtadir, M.A. and E. Denison Ross (1921). *Catalogue of the Arabic and Persian Manuscripts in the Oriental Library at Bankipore*, vol. VII. Calcutta.

Mutribi (1977). *Khatirat-i Mutribi Samarqandi*, ed. Abdul Ghani Mirzoyef. Karachi.

Okada, Amina (n.d.). *Imperial Mughal Painters: Indian Miniatures from the Sixteenth and Seventeenth Centuries*. Flammarion.

Pal, Pratapaditya (ed.) (1972). *Aspects of Indian Art*. Leiden.

——————— (1983). *Court Paintings of India, 16th–19th Centuries*. New York.

——————— (ed.) (1991). *Master Artists of the Imperial Mughal Court*. Bombay.

——————— (1993). *Indian Painting: A Catalogue of the Los Angeles Country Museum of Art Collection*, vol. 1 (1000–1700). California.

Payne, C.H. (1926). *Akbar and the Jesuits*. London.

——————— (1930). *Jahangir and the Jesuits*. London.

Pelsaert, Francisco, '*Remonstratie*' (1626), tr. W. Moreland and Geyl (1925) as *Jahangir's India*. Cambridge (reprint: 1972, Delhi).

Qaiser Ahsan Jan (1982). *The Indian Response to European Technology and Culture (AD 1498–1707)*. Delhi.

Qaiser Ahsan Jan and S.P. Verma (eds) (1993). *Art and Culture: Felicitation Volume in Honour of Professor S. Nurul Hasan*. Jaipur.

——————— (eds) (1996). *Art and Culture: Endeavours in Interpretation*. New Delhi.

——————— (eds) (2002). *Art and Culture: Painting and Perspective*. New Delhi.

Qandhari Haji Muhammad 'Arif (1972). *Ta'rikh-i Akbari* (1580), ed. Imtiyaz Ali Arshi. Rampur.

Qazi Ahmad (1959). *Calligraphers and Painters (dated AH 1015) (AD 1606)*, tr. into Russian from the Persian text by V. Minorsky with an introduction by B.N. Jabhoder; tr. from Russian text into English by T. Minorsky. Washington.

Qazwini, Mulla 'Alaud-Daula (1573). *Nafa'is-al Ma'asir*, MAL, MS, Aligarh Muslim University.

Randhawa, M.S. (1983). *Paintings of the Baburnama*, National Museum, New Delhi.

Rawson, Philip S. (1961). *Indian Painting*. London.

Ray, Niharranjan (1975). *Mughal Court Painting*. Calcutta.

Robinson, B.W. (1953). *The Kevorkian Collection: Islamic and Indian MSS, Miniature Paintings and Drawings*. New Delhi.

——————— (ed.) (1976). *Islamic Painting and the Arts of the Book (The Keir Collection)*. London.

Rogers, J.M. (1993). *Mughal Miniatures*. London.

Shah Nawaz Khan, *Ma'asir ul Umara'* (1742–80), ed. Abdu'r Rahim and Ashraf Ali, Bib. Ind., Calcutta, tr. H. Beveridge (1911), Bib. Ind., Calcutta.

Swanti Swarup (1983). *Flora and Fauna in Mughal Art.* Bombay.

Smith, V.A. (1911). *A History of Fine Art in India and Ceylon.* Oxford.

Stchoukine, I. (1929a). *La Peinture Indienne a l'Epoque des Grands Moghols.* Paris.

——————— (1929b). *Les Miniatures, Indiennes de l'Epoque des Grands Moghols du Musee de Louvre.* Paris.

Stronge, Susan (2002). *Painting for the Mughal Emperor: The Art of the Book 1560–1660.* London.

——————— (2010). *Made for Mughal Emperors: Royal Treasures from Hindustan.* New Delhi.

Suleiman, H. (1970). *Miniatures of the Baburnama.* Tashkent.

Tavernier, Jean Baptiste (1925). *Travels in India,* tr. V. Bali, ed. W. Crooke. London.

Thevenot, M. de (1949). *Indian Travels of Thevenot and Careri,* ed. S. Sen. New Delhi.

Titley, Norah M. (1977). *Miniatures from Persian Manuscripts (A catalogue and subject index of paintings from Persia, India and Turkey in the British Library and the British Museum).* London.

Verma, S.P. (1978). *Art and Material Culture in the Paintings of Akbar's Court.* New Delhi.

Verma, S.P. (1994). *Mughal Painters and Their Work: A Bibliographical Survey and Comprehensive Catalogue*. New Delhi.

——————— (1999). *Mughal Painter of Flora and Fauna, Ustad Mansur*. New Delhi.

——————— (ed.) (1999). *Flora and Fauna in Mughal Art*. Mumbai.

——————— (2005). *Painting: The Mughal Experience*. New Delhi.

——————— (2009). *Interpreting Mughal Painting: Essays on Art, Society, and Culture*. New Delhi.

——————— (2011). *Crossing Cultural Frontiers: Biblical Themes in Mughal Painting*. New Delhi.

Welch, S.C. (1963). *The Art of Mughal India: Painting and Precious Objects (Catalogue of an exhibition shown in the galleries of Asia House, New York during the winter of 1964)*. New York.

——————— (1973). *A Flower From Every Meadow: Indian Painting From American Collections (Catalogue of the exhibition shown in the galleries of Asia House, New York, 1973)*. New York.

——————— (1976). *Indian Drawings and Painted Sketches (16th through 19th Centuries)*. New York.

——————— (1978). *Imperial Mughal Painting*. London.

——————— (1985). *Art and Sculpture (1300–1900), Catalogue of the exhibition 'India' held at the Metropolitan Museum of Art from September 14, 1985 to January 5, 1986)*. New York.

Welch, S.C. and M.C. Beach (1965). *Gods, Thrones and Peacocks (Catalogue of an exhibition held in Asia House Gallery, New York, from 23rd September to 12th December, 1965; Baltimore Museum of Art, from 18th January to 27th February and Munson-Williams-Proctor Institute, Utica, New York, from 3rd April to 15th May, 1966)*. New York.

Welch, S.C., A. Schimmel, M.L. Swietochowski, and W.M. Thackston (1987). *The Emperors' Album, Images of Mughal India*. New York.

Wilkinson, J.V.S. (1948). *Mughal Painting*. London.

Index

Haldar, Asit Kumar (artist,
    Bengal school), 149
halo, 69–70
Hamzanama, art of,
    xxv, xxxix, xl–xliii,
    xlvii–xlviii, li–lii, 5, 25;
    division of visual field,
    31–2, 37; paintings of
    women, 79; margin
    illustration, 115;
    influence of European
    art, 133
Harivansha, xix, xxv
Hashim (or Mir Hashim)
    (Mughal painter), xxxi,
    23, 71
Hashim Haini
    (superintendent of
    Humayun's library),
    xxii, 3
Havell, E.B., comment on
    Bichitr's work, 66
Humayun, his painters
    at Kabul xxi–xxii;
    bestowed upon Abdu-s
    Samad the title *Shirin
    Qalam*, xxxvi; his atelier,
    liv, 3

Husaini (Mughal painter),
    125
Hyus, P. (Flemish artist), 134

Ibrahim Adil Khan, portrait
    of, xxxi
Ibrahim Kashmiri (Mughal
    painter), 24
Ibrahim Lahori (Mughal
    painter), 24
Ikhlas (Mughal painter),
    125
Ilyas Bahadur (Mughal
    painter, of Aurangzeb's
    reign), 11
Ilyas Khan (Mughal painter,
    of Aurangzeb's reign), 11
'Inayat (Mughal painter), 98
Itimaduddaula, *Jahangirnama*
    gifted to him, 47
'*Iyar-i Danish*, 93

Jagan (Mughal painter), 20
Jahangir, interest in painting;
    passion for exotic
    nature and wildlife,
    xxvi–xxvi; his atelier,
    xxix; recognition and